IN
SEARCH
OF
WISDOM

LIFE-CHANGING
Truths in the Book
of Proverbs

JOYCE MEYER

FaithWords

New York • Nashville

FaithWords
Hachette Book Group
1290 Avenue of the Americas, New York, NY 10104
faithwords.com
twitter.com/faithwords

First Edition: January 2021

FaithWords is a division of Hachette Book Group, Inc.

The FaithWords name and logo are trademarks of Hachette Book Group, Inc.

The publisher is not responsible for websites (or their content) that are not owned by the publisher.

The Hachette Speakers Bureau provides a wide range of authors for speaking events. To find out more, go to www.hachettespeakersbureau.com or call (866) 376-6591.

Unless otherwise noted, Scripture quotations are taken from the Holy Bible, New International Version®, NIV®. Copyright ©1973, 1978, 1984, 2011 by Biblica, Inc.™ Used by permission of Zondervan. All rights reserved worldwide. www.zondervan.com The "NIV" and "New International Version" are trademarks registered in the United States Patent and Trademark Office by Biblica, Inc.™

Scripture quotations marked AMPC are taken from the Amplified® Bible, Copyright © 1954, 1958, 1962, 1964, 1965, 1987 by The Lockman Foundation. Used by permission. www.Lockman.org. | Scripture quotations marked KJV are taken from the King James Version of the Bible. | Scripture quotations marked NKJV are taken from the New King James Version®. Copyright © 1982 by Thomas Nelson. Used by permission. All rights reserved. | Scripture quotations marked AMP are taken from the Amplified® Bible, Copyright © 2015 by The Lockman Foundation. Used by permission. www.Lockman.org. | Scriptures indicated from the Good News Bible are taken from the Good News Translation—Second Edition © 1992 by American Bible Society. Used by permission. | Scripture quotations marked ESV are taken from The Holy Bible, English Standard Version. ESV® Text Edition: 2016. Copyright © 2001 by Crossway Bibles, a publishing ministry of Good News Publishers. | Scripture quotations marked NLT are taken from the Holy Bible, New Living Translation, copyright ©1996, 2004, 2007, 2013, 2015 by Tyndale House Foundation. Used by permission of Tyndale House Publishers, Inc., Carol Stream, Illinois 60188. All rights reserved.

Library of Congress Cataloging-in-Publication Data

Names: Meyer, Joyce, author.
Title: In search of wisdom : life-changing truths in the Book of Proverbs / Joyce Meyer.
Description: New York : FaithWords, 2021.
Identifiers: LCCN 2020030165 | ISBN 9781546017646 (hardcover) | ISBN 9781546015611 (large type) | ISBN 9781546017639 (ebook) Subjects: LCSH: Bible. Proverbs--Criticism, interpretation, etc. Classification: LCC BS1465.52 .M49 2021 | DDC 223/.706--dc23 LC record available at https://lccn.loc.gov/2020030165

Printed in the United States of America

LSC-H

Printing 1, 2020

CONTENTS

INTRODUCTION

The Book of Proverbs is considered the Bible's book of wisdom, and it deals with both the practical and the spiritual issues of life. Wisdom is one of the greatest assets we can possess, and in order to have it, we must seek it diligently. Wisdom is simply the proper use of knowledge, and I like to define it as "doing now what we will be happy with later in life." If we do as God instructs each day, then our tomorrows will be pleasing to Him and pleasant for us.

Each chapter of Proverbs is filled with principles that will benefit us if we obey them. I know numerous people whose lives are now falling apart because they have not made wise decisions in the past. Had they lived according to the principles Proverbs teaches, they would have none of their current problems, and their lives would be prosperous, peaceful, happy, and fruitful. When we search for wisdom and apply it to our lives, we will enjoy blessing, peace, joy, and fulfillment. We will be a blessing to others and live a life that is pleasing to God.

Proverbs contains thirty-one chapters. The Old Testament king Solomon wrote the first twenty-nine of them, with the exception of 22:17 through the end of chapter 24, which were written by two sages. A sage was a man, often elderly, who possessed wisdom beyond that of ordinary people. A man named Agur wrote chapter 30, and King Lemuel wrote chapter 31. It's interesting to note that King Solomon and the other writers of Proverbs did not sit down and write all of these wise sayings in a short time, but that the book was compiled over a period of perhaps as many as two hundred years. This assures us that its wisdom has been tried and proven.

Proverbs includes teaching on how to treat people; wisdom; knowledge; understanding; discretion; discernment; prudence; the fear of the Lord; how to think; the importance of words; how to manage finances and the importance of staying out of debt; how to behave in marriage; cultivating good relationships; how to handle offenses, correction, and discipline; having a happy heart; anger; laziness; attitude; generosity; honesty; work; poverty; greed; and more. I do not intend for this book to address every subject mentioned in all thirty-one chapters of Proverbs. Instead, in each chapter of this book, I will focus and expound on several principles from the corresponding chapter in Proverbs, principles that I believe will greatly help you manage your daily life and obtain and grow in wisdom.

In order to follow the wisdom Proverbs offers, we need to be willing to obey God's Word no matter how we feel, what we think, or what we want. This simply means that walking in wisdom requires spiritual maturity. Proverbs helps us gain that maturity as we learn its principles and secure God's help to practice them. The search for wisdom is a journey, and having its principles worked into our character and become our natural responses to the issues of life requires time, thought, and practice.

Throughout this book I will ask you some questions about the lessons Proverbs teaches. These are easy yes-or-no questions I've included simply to inspire you to think and to ask yourself how you are living relative to the principle being taught in a specific section of the book. These questions will also help you determine whether you are following wisdom. Reading about and knowing biblical principles is good, but knowledge that does not lead to action will not help you on a practical level. The questions will help keep you from merely reading Proverbs abstractly without applying its teachings to your life. They are not meant to make you feel uncomfortable, but to prompt you to apply what you are reading so that if you need help in the area to which a question pertains, you will allow the truth to make you free.

If you want to incorporate God's Word into your daily life, which is God's desire, this study of Proverbs will be very beneficial to you. In looking at other books written on Proverbs, I found a variety of ways to approach the process of writing this book. I kept feeling drawn to write about this book of the Bible, but I lacked clarity regarding how to go about it because it covers so many different subjects. In addition, many of the same topics are covered in several chapters. I settled on writing one chapter of this book on each chapter of Proverbs. Some chapters are longer than others, and my prayer has been that the Holy Spirit would guide me concerning what to highlight in each one.

As you read this book, I strongly suggest that you read the entire chapter of Proverbs to which each chapter pertains. The text of the Book of Proverbs is included in this book to aid you in this study. I pray you will be enlightened with God's wisdom and His ways as we begin this journey through Proverbs and as we search for wisdom together.

SEVEN FOUNDATIONAL PRINCIPLES

As we begin our study of Proverbs, I believe that defining and gaining understanding of the seven key words or phrases used frequently throughout its thirty-one chapters is vital. These seven principles are interwoven into many of the principles that Proverbs presents, principles that should guide our actions in everyday life. Knowing what these terms mean is foundational to understanding and applying the whole of the message God wants to teach us through the Book of Proverbs.

The first five verses of Proverbs instruct us to seek and gain wisdom, understanding, prudence, knowledge, discretion, and discernment. We are also to walk in the fear of the Lord. It is easy to skim these opening verses without genuinely understanding the immensity of what the writer communicates. Let me give you some simple definitions of these words to expand your understanding of what they truly mean.

Wisdom
One word for *wisdom* is the Hebrew word *chokmah*, which is used often in Proverbs and refers to the knowledge and

ability to make the right choice at the right time. The prerequisite for this wisdom is the fear of the Lord.

Wisdom is both an Old Testament and a New Testament principle. Two primary New Testament Greek words translated as *wisdom* are *sophia* and *phronesis*. *Sophia* is true insight into the nature of things, and *phronesis* is wise action "derived from learning," according to the Oxford Review. *Sophia* is theoretical, and *phronesis* is practical. In my opinion, we look at far too many things in theory without applying them practically in our daily lives. Everything God says is good and worth hearing, but if we do not apply it to our lives, it does not benefit us or anyone else.

We are instructed to *do* God's Word, not merely to hear it (James 1:22). The fact that so many people hear the Word without acting on it is probably one of the biggest problems in Christianity today. We are often proud of what we know, yet we fail to act on it, which causes our witness to the world to be impotent and meaningless.

Understanding

Understanding refers to the rational rather than the emotional, and it is closely linked to *knowledge*. Understanding something means we "get it" or grasp its meaning deeply enough to cause us to realize the importance of taking action according to what we know. Understanding is to be acquired, sought after, and learned. It requires not only meditation on a subject, but an examination of actions taken in order to fully comprehend the result of those actions. For example, we may understand the impact of our words only after we

ruin a relationship through being excessively critical of someone. Or, we may understand the benefit of encouragement
and compliments only after watching them heal a broken
relationship.

Prudence

Prudence is forethought (thinking ahead) and foresight (seeing ahead). It is also the ability to use reason to govern and
discipline ourselves. To be prudent is to live with the mindset
of managing our resources and life's affairs well. Although
prudence itself does not perform any action and is related
to knowledge and the way we think, the virtue of prudence
controls all other virtues.

Just think about how many people do not manage their
resources or other issues of life well. They often do what feels
good at the moment without any forethought about how a
current action will affect them in the future. Have you ever
seen a person who eats mostly unhealthy, nutritionally deficient food; eats excessively; gets no exercise; and wakes up
one day skinny? Or have you ever seen someone who buys
everything they want, has multiple credit cards that all carry
maximum balances, is wasteful, won't work, and doesn't pay
their debts and then wakes up one morning as a multimil-
lionaire? Of course we have not seen these things, because
they cannot occur.

Only through prudence and good management of our
resources will we prosper and then reach results we can enjoy.
This holds true for every area of life.

Knowledge

The Hebrew word for knowledge is *yada*, which appears approximately 950 times in Scripture and conveys a much broader meaning than our English word *knowledge*. It includes perceiving, learning, understanding, willing, performing, and experiencing. To *know* is not to be intellectually informed about some abstract principle, but to apprehend and experience its reality. It is not the possession of information, but rather its exercise or realization.

An example of this would be what it means to *know* God's love. This refers to knowing His love deeply, intimately, and experientially in a deeply personal way. It is much more than mere mental ascent.

Discretion

Discretion is the quality of behaving or speaking in such a way as to avoid causing offense or revealing private information. A discreet person can be counted on to keep another's secrets. Those who use discretion concerning their words are effective at communicating clearly and meaningfully with others. Even when they need to correct someone, they bring correction in a way that enables the other person to accept what is being said. Some synonyms for *discretion* are *circumspection*, *delicacy*, *discernment*, and *prudence*.

A discreet friend is very valuable. At Joyce Meyer Ministries, our staff pastor is excellent at conflict resolution because he uses discretion as he arbitrates disagreements between individuals.

Discernment

To discern means to distinguish or separate so as to investigate; to examine, scrutinize, or question. People with discernment can judge between good and evil and between right and wrong. They take time to see beyond the surface of people and situations into the true nature of someone or something. Discerning between good and evil spirits is one of the nine gifts of the Holy Spirit (1 Corinthians 12:10).

I think discernment is one of the most valuable character traits we can develop and one of the most beneficial gifts that God gives us. The world today is filled with deception, and many things are not as they seem on the surface. Through God's grace and goodness, we can learn not to judge according to what we see with our natural eyes or hear with our natural ears, but we can spiritually discern the true nature of a person or set of circumstances.

The Fear of the Lord

This is perhaps one of the most misunderstood phrases in the Bible. We are not to be afraid of the Lord, as the word *fear* would indicate in today's usage, for He is good and would never harm us. However, we should have a reverential fear and worshipful awe of the mighty God we serve. Moses told the Israelites that the fear of God would keep them from sinning (Exodus 20:20), and I wholeheartedly agree. One minister said, "It is a sovereign respect for God that makes us dread above all other things to offend Him."

The fear of the Lord is the "beginning of knowledge"

(Proverbs 1:7). In other words, we cannot learn anything else He wants to teach us unless we first walk in and understand the reverential fear of God.

God is our friend, but we must never forget that He is Almighty God. He is the God whose presence causes people to lie prostrate, and to fall to the ground face down in abject humility. In the Bible, people such as Moses, Aaron, Abram, Joshua, the disciples, wise men from the East at Christ's birth (called Magi in the NIV), and even Jesus Himself fell before the Lord in reverential fear (Numbers 20:6; Genesis 17:3; Joshua 5:14; Matthew 17:6; 2:11; 26:39). Even angels and the idol named Dagon fall before God (Revelation 7:11; 1 Samuel 5:3). The Bible speaks of the "kindness and sternness of God" (Romans 11:22). He is a just God who makes wrong things right, and He is a merciful and forgiving God, but He is also a God who, in His love, corrects us for our own good when we need to be corrected.

* * *

Understanding the meanings of these seven words and phrases is vital to making the most of our study of Proverbs. Each requires an investment of time. Wisdom waits, discretion and discernment must wait and listen before taking action, and the type of understanding and knowledge spoken of in Proverbs requires waiting and searching. If we desire these qualities to operate in our lives, we must commit to slowing down. We will need to stop multitasking and learn to enjoy times of solitude and blessed quiet to think sincerely and thoroughly about actions we will take, remembering that each action produces a result.

As you go through this book, let me encourage you to look for the seven foundational principles I have mentioned, learning all you can learn about each one and about the other topics addressed in Proverbs. May God bless you in your search for wisdom.

PROVERBS 1

Proverbs 1 begins by mentioning the seven foundational principles listed in the introduction to this book. Then, verse 7 ends with the statement "but fools despise wisdom and instruction." The NIV footnote for Proverbs 1:7 says, "The Hebrew words rendered *fool* in Proverbs, and often elsewhere in the Old Testament, denote *a person who is morally deficient*" (emphasis mine). Proverbs includes many references to foolish people, so I encourage you to keep this definition in mind as you read through this book.

If I were to write my own definition of a fool, it would be this: A fool is morally deficient, hasty in making decisions, and too quick to speak without thinking. He is probably not prudent with finances and makes poor decisions in all areas of life. He thinks more highly of himself than he should. He is probably lazy and does not exercise self-control. He has an attitude of entitlement, thinking he should be given what he has not worked for or earned. I am sure he lacks appreciation and is ungrateful. He most likely murmurs and complains regularly. He gossips, falls in with bad company, and has no reverential fear and awe of God.

PARENTS CAN BE SOURCES OF WISDOM

Proverbs 1 continues by urging children to listen to the instructions of their fathers and not to forsake the teaching of their mothers (v. 8). Many of us would not have been wise to heed the advice we received from our parents if they were walking in the ways of the world and were ungodly. That was the case with me, but thankfully my real Father—my heavenly Father—has taught and continues to teach me how to live. I am learning more and more all the time about the wisdom of listening to Him.

If you had good parents who truly loved you and the Lord, I hope you will rejoice, because you had a gift that many people don't have the opportunity to benefit from or enjoy. Young people commonly go through a phase when they feel certain their parents are totally out of touch with reality and know absolutely nothing of relevance. Of course, this is wrong thinking that hopefully will be corrected in a short period of time, because a wise person learns everything possible from wise, godly people, especially older ones. The longer we live, the more experiences we have; therefore, the more we know experientially. Experiential knowledge is not the same as factual knowledge, and it leads to wisdom, not simply to information.

> *Do you listen intently when those who are older and have more life experience than you do offer advice, or do you merely assume they cannot relate to you because of their age?*

Most parents have done certain things right and certain things wrong. They have experienced the results of wise and unwise decisions, and they deeply desire to help their children avoid the mistakes they have made. Solomon says the teaching of our parents can be viewed as a fine piece of jewelry to adorn our necks (v. 9). Or, if you prefer, a prized possession for which we should be thankful.

THE ENTICEMENT OF SINFUL PEOPLE

Many good people have been ruined by the influence of sinful people around them, and Proverbs urges and warns us to not fall into their trap. The writer says, "If sinful men entice you, do not give in to them" (v. 10). Verses 10–15 teach us that the ungodly don't give up easily. They keep enticing by telling lies and promising rewards that actually are a myth. They try to make us believe that if we take advantage of others to serve ourselves, we will gain all sorts of valuable things. Those of us who have experience with sin know for certain that wrongdoing does not bring anything valuable. We can hear the father's pleading heart in verse 15 when he says, "My son, do not go along with them, do not set your foot on their paths."

How good are you at saying no to things that look exciting and enjoyable when you know that God does not approve of them? These are sinful enticements, and Satan works through sinful people to draw godly men and women away from the right (godly) path onto the wrong (ungodly) path. These people may be such experts in convincing others to follow them that even the godliest individual may drift onto the wrong path in life and not even know how it happened. This is the reason 1 Peter 5:9 instructs us to resist the devil at "his onset," meaning when he first begins to lead us astray (AMPC).

Jesus says that if our eye causes us to sin, we should pluck it out of our head. And if our arm causes us to sin, we should remove it from our body because "It is better for you to lose one part of your body than for your whole body to go into hell" (Matthew 5:29–30). In this current, so-called modern age, do we deal harshly enough with sin, or do we compromise and assume casual attitudes toward sin, believing that God's grace will cover us because He is good?

Sometimes, out of loneliness, Christians become involved with certain people and realize they simply don't have peace about those relationships. Many times this is because those people want to tempt us to sin or to draw us away from God. It is easy to make excuses and justify wrong behavior, but there is no true justification for doing what we know God would have us not do.

Sinful people rush to evil, and "they are swift to shed blood" (v. 16) but "they ambush only themselves!" (v. 18). This is a powerful thought. It emphasizes the biblical principle that people reap what they sow (Galatians 6:7). No one can sow evil and reap good.

Sinful people pursue "ill-gotten gain" (things they obtain through dishonesty), whether they steal possessions, money or investments, or ideas or intellectual property. Any kind of illegal gain eventually "takes away" their lives (v. 19). Just think about it. If people steal, they will probably go to prison, or at least feel crushed under the burden of guilt they carry in their hearts while pretending to be happy. They forfeit the life God wants them to have through their own foolishness. Material goods gained from sinful actions may seem appealing in the beginning but are ultimately empty and unfulfilling.

It's important to realize that stealing is not limited to money, property, or possessions. People have also had their ideas or intellectual property stolen, and when someone commits plagiarism, they are stealing someone else's writings.

Some inventors have even had their ideas stolen before they could apply for patents. For example, when you think of a sewing machine, the first brand name that probably comes to mind is Singer. This company has long been associated with sewing machines, and remains probably the most recognizable name in sewing today. But Isaac Singer actually stole the idea for the sewing machine from a man named Elias Howe. In 1854, Howe sued the company for royalties—and won.

WISDOM CALLS OUT

As we continue in Proverbs 1, wisdom begins to take on the qualities of an actual living entity, speaking and expounding on the benefits of listening to her. Of course, wisdom is God or God's Word, but I like that it is presented as a person who is teaching us how to live. You will notice that wisdom is referred to as "she." Throughout Scripture, aspects and attributes of God are described using both masculine and feminine terms. Here, wisdom is personified in a feminine way.

When I read Proverbs 1:20–33, I see in my mind's eye a picture of wisdom at the intersections of our lives, crying out, "Listen to me!" She "calls aloud, she raises her voice in the public square" (v. 20). Then comes the question, "How long will you who are simple love your simple ways?" (v. 22). Today we might urge people to "simplify" their lives, but the Hebrew word used for *simple* in Proverbs carries a different meaning than the contemporary English word *simple*. To the writer of Proverbs, a simple person was "gullible, without moral direction and inclined to evil."

These people did not listen to wisdom, and I am sure they were very dissatisfied with their lives. After beseeching the simple to listen to her, wisdom instructs people to "repent at my rebuke!" (v. 23).

How easy it is to quickly glide over those four words, but they speak volumes to us if we truly listen. Thank God for the gift of repentance. How marvelous it is that we may repent, which means to turn and go in the opposite direction and receive forgiveness and a new beginning. Wisdom does not rebuke us to make us feel guilty, but to urge us to make a positive change in God's direction.

If we are willing to repent when we are rebuked (scolded or reprimanded), we will gain more wisdom and understand how to follow it. Wisdom reflects God's thoughts and teachings, and it is something we should all desire because without

God's thoughts and understanding we will make many painful mistakes.

Wisdom also speaks to the mockers and asks how long they will delight in their mockery (v. 22). To mock is to make light of, to disregard, or to laugh at. We should never take any of God's commands or principles lightly, disregarding them or joking about them. People who walk in the reverential fear of God will refrain from any kind of mockery.

I'm sure you can see as we begin our study of Proverbs that the seven key principles I mentioned in the introduction are indeed intermingled throughout this book. We learned that the fear of God is the beginning of wisdom and that it prevents us from sinning. Now we see that those who "delight in mockery" will only cease their ridicule if they have the reverential fear of God.

WISDOM'S RESPONSE TO THOSE WHO REFUSE TO LISTEN

Wisdom declares the future for those who refuse to listen to her, saying, "Since you disregard all my advice and do not accept my rebuke, I in turn will laugh when disaster strikes you" (vv. 25–26). I realize this sounds stern, but it is what God's Word says, and we cannot blame Him when troubles come because we have refused to listen to wise counsel. Many people who are not making good choices and living in obedience to God are not very interested in hearing about what the outcome of their current actions will be. In Proverbs

1:25–29, wisdom speaks plainly about what will happen to the simple who refuse to listen to her. She says that disaster will sweep over them, calamity will overtake them, and trouble will overwhelm them. Then, when they call on God for help, He won't answer! He says He will not respond because "they hated knowledge and did not choose to fear the Lord" (v. 29).

This scenario describes what will happen to the unrepentant, but the person who listens to wisdom's rebuke and repents has the opportunity for a new beginning. Thank God we can always begin again. No matter how we have behaved in the past, if we are sincerely sorry

> Is listening to and following wisdom a priority in your life?

for our misdeeds and repent of them, God instantly forgives us and even forgets our sins completely (Isaiah 43:25; Hebrews 8:12). Even though God promises us total forgiveness and new beginnings, it is always better to do what is right to begin with. If we do, we avoid much guilt, confusion, failure, and misery.

Everything God tells us is only for our good. I urge you to believe that and decide to start really listening to His voice with the intention of acting on what you learn from His Word.

According to Proverbs, those who "eat the fruit of their ways" are warned once again that the "waywardness of the simple will kill them," but whoever listens to wisdom (God's Word) "will live in safety and be at ease, without fear of harm" (vv. 31–33). Wow! This is what we all want, and Proverbs 1 gives us the roadmap that will lead us straight to it.

PROVERBS 2

Proverbs 2 speaks about the moral benefits of wisdom. Of course, as I mentioned in chapter 1, wisdom is God or God's Word, and it is presented as a person who is trying to teach and help us. In Proverbs 2:1–5, we see several of the seven foundational principles mentioned again—wisdom (v. 2), understanding (v. 2), the fear of the Lord (v. 5), and knowledge (v. 5). We read that if we will listen to wisdom and search for insight and understanding, as we would search for silver and hidden treasure, that we "will understand the fear of the Lord and find the knowledge of God" (v. 5). God seems to like to hide things to see if we are interested enough to do the work of finding them. Think about it like this: God provides gold, silver, and precious stones for beautiful jewelry and many other things. He provides iron, copper, and other metals for us to use in building and producing other products we use, but someone has to dig for them. They are hidden in hills and mountains, and they are deep within the ground. God provides the treasure, but we have to do the digging.

In many undeveloped countries, people walk miles each day just to get filthy, disease-ridden water from a river or pond. According to the World Health Organization, water-borne illness kills 3.4 million people each year, including four thousand children each day. What's tragic is that the villages in which these people live have clean, healthy water in the ground beneath them, but no one knows how to dig it out. Joyce Meyer Ministries has been privileged to provide the equipment and technology to dig more than 1,500 clean water wells in some of the most remote places on earth. This brings people to Jesus because they see His love being extended to them, and that changes their lives. God had already provided what they needed, but they didn't dig for it. Wisdom wants us to dig, seek, search, cry out, and listen to her. As we are diligent to find wisdom, we will enjoy a blessed life and will have the opportunity to bless those around us.

Let me encourage you to be diligent in all endeavors, not complacent or passive. Passive people want something good to happen to them, thinking they will sit and do nothing while waiting to see if it does. But that is not the way to a successful and enjoyable life. We are partners with God. He has a part to play, and we cannot do His part no matter how hard we try. We also have a part to play, and God won't do our part no matter how much we would like Him to. He gives us the knowledge and strength to do what we need to do, but we must choose to take action and do it.

God does certain things for us with no effort on our part. For example, salvation is available to us by His grace, not because of works we have done to deserve it (Ephesians 2:8–9). Mercy cannot be earned or deserved, and forgiveness of our sins is a gift from God. But we still need to ask, and ask in faith, in order to receive them. God wants us to avoid *works of the flesh* (things we try to do in our own strength that only He can do). He does not want us to avoid work itself, but that is different than engaging in works of the flesh.

God has gifted me to teach His Word. I couldn't do it without Him, but He doesn't do all of the work for me. I still study, develop messages, and go over them many times, making sure I have done my part before I step onto a platform expecting God to do His part. I work, but I don't get into works of the flesh (self-effort apart from God's leading and grace) and become frustrated about the work I am doing. I do my part and trust God to do His part.

The idea that God provides but that we still need to be active and do what He gives us to do started in the Garden of Eden and runs throughout His Word:

> The Lord God took the man and put him in the Garden of Eden to work it and take care of it.
>
> Genesis 2:15

God provided the garden, and He gave Adam the ability to take care of it. But Adam had to choose to follow God's instructions:

> All hard work brings a profit, but mere talk leads only to poverty.
>
> Proverbs 14:23

Throughout Proverbs we find that passivity, laziness, and an unwillingness to work hard cause problems. We are to be committed, diligent, and willing to work. Every effort we sow according to God's purpose and plan for us will bring an abundant harvest into our lives.

SUCCESS AND PROTECTION

Proverbs teaches us that God "holds success in store for the upright" (v. 7). Let's be clear about what being successful means. It is not primarily about having a lot of money or a high position at work or in the community. Success is first having a close, intimate relationship with God through Christ. Then it entails an abundance of peace and joy, regardless of our circumstances.

The Oxford dictionary says that the definition of *success* is the attainment of popularity or profit, but God defines *success* differently. Although successful people will have their needs met and have enough left over to bless others, not all people who are successful will be millionaires or CEOs. I believe that to be successful in God's eyes, we need pure hearts, an intense love for Him and for people, a desire to serve, and an eagerness to learn and grow spiritually.

Yes, God promises success to the upright, but being upright does not mean we are perfect. It does mean that we *want* to be perfect because of our love for Jesus, and that we are willing to press toward that goal as long as we live.

Wisdom also promises to shield "those whose walk is blameless," whose course in life is just, and whose way is faithful (vv. 7–8). The promise of God's protection is often repeated in Scripture and is very comforting. The world today is extremely violent, and I would much rather know that God is protecting me than to think I had to be on guard, constantly trying to protect myself. We read in Proverbs 2:11–12 that wisdom saves us, and discretion will protect and guard us. It especially says that wisdom will save us from people whose "words are perverse" and who "walk in dark ways" and "delight in doing wrong" (vv. 12–14).

The people we choose as our friends and companions in life are very important because they influence us more than we may realize. However, if we operate in wisdom, which is the proper use of knowledge or doing now what we will be satisfied with later, it will protect us from people who will influence us negatively by guiding us to avoid them.

UNFAITHFULNESS

"You shall not commit adultery" is one of the Ten Commandments God gave Moses to give to the Israelites (Exodus 20:14). Proverbs 2:16 is Proverbs' first mention of adultery, but not the last, as the writer of Proverbs issues many warnings against sexual immorality. In Proverbs 2:16–19, the adulterous woman speaks seductive words, she has ignored the covenant she made before God when she married, and her house leads to death.

> *Do you have friends who build you up and make you better, or ones who tear you down and have no good influence on you?*

Sexual sin is probably ranked high on the scale of sins

most often committed. This tells me that temptation in this area is very strong, at least for many people. Every sin does not yield the same degree of destruction. Adultery brings a special kind of misery because it hurts many people and is said to be a sin against one's own body (1 Corinthians 6:18). When a man and a woman enter into a sexual relationship, it creates a bond between them, because in that relationship, the two become one. In addition, our bodies belong to the Lord and we are to glorify and honor Him through them (1 Corinthians 6:19–20).

If we follow wisdom, it will cause us to keep to the right path in life. Faithful people "walk in the ways of good," but "the unfaithful will be torn from" the land (vv. 20, 22). Sexual temptation can be very compelling, but the momentary pleasure it may bring is not worth the destruction and trouble it causes.

Many people think about wisdom in terms of how they spend their time or money, or in regard to practical decisions regarding their future. But wisdom is also vitally important in relationships and in personal matters, as we see in the comments Proverbs 2 makes about adultery. In every area of your life, be wise and do now what you will be happy with later.

PROVERBS 3

The NIV heading for Proverbs 3 is "Wisdom Bestows Well-Being." This is certainly true, and therefore we are encouraged not to forget the teaching of wisdom, because it will prolong our lives for many years and bring us "peace and prosperity" (vv. 1–2). It stands to reason that if we use wisdom concerning our bodies, we position ourselves to live longer lives. How many people shorten their lives due to years and years of eating junk food, failing to get enough sleep or rest, not drinking enough water, and ignoring the need for exercise? Add to this an overload of stress and schedules that force us to multitask and hurry almost constantly, and it is no wonder many people feel bad physically and mentally, and even die prematurely simply because they did not use wisdom regarding their health.

BE SATISFIED NOT KNOWING

Proverbs 3:3–6 is one of my favorite Bible passages. It teaches us to trust God and not to rely on our own understanding, but to submit to God in all of our ways. If we follow this wise advice, He will direct and make straight the path before us.

When we lean on our own understanding, we often fall into reasoning—rotating our minds around and around a subject, wanting to know who, what, when, where, and how. Reasoning causes most of us a lot of frustration and confusion. I know that the more I reason, the more confused I become. The rule I have for myself concerning reasoning is that I am free to think about a situation, ponder it, and ask God to reveal hidden things to me, but when I am getting no answer from God and becoming confused instead, then it is time to cast my care on God and be satisfied not knowing the answers I have tried to figure out.

If God withholds knowledge from us, He has a good reason for doing so. If nothing else, His silence serves as an opportunity for us to grow in learning to trust Him. I was once the type of person who wanted to know every reason behind everything. I came to realize I was addicted to reasoning; I could not settle down and be content unless I thought I had all the answers. Eventually, God's grace set me free from the drive to know so much. I discovered that sometimes the less I know, the happier I am. Trusting God and not leaning on my own understanding is the best stress reliever I know of.

Proverbs 3:7 encourages us not to be wise in our own eyes. This verse confronts us with the need for humility. We often think we can handle situations on our own because we think we are far more capable than we are. But God knows that apart from Him we can do nothing (John 15:5). We can do all things through Him, but nothing without Him (Philippians 4:13). God's Word advises us not to think more highly of ourselves than we should (Romans 12:3). If we follow this instruction and humbly depend on the Lord in all situations, we will avoid a great deal of misery and experience His blessings in our lives.

THE FEAR OF THE LORD

The writer of Proverbs once again brings up the subject of the fear of the Lord and informs us that fearing God and avoiding evil will bring health to our bodies and nourishment to our bones (vv. 7–8). Simply put, we will be healthier if we shun evil and maintain a healthy reverential fear and awe of God. Scripture makes clear that if we follow God's advice, our lives will be enjoyable, successful, and fruitful, but if we don't, we will experience unhappiness and misery in our bodies, souls, spirits, and daily lives.

I am not suggesting that we should cower before God or fear that He will harm us if we make a mistake, but we should recognize and revere His holiness and His power. Hebrews 12:29 says, "God is a consuming fire." As I look at society today and see the loose morals of even many Christians, I feel we need a healthy dose of the proper reverential fear and awe of God. The person who reverently fears the Lord would rather do anything than offend Him!

BRING YOUR FIRSTFRUITS TO GOD

Proverbs 3:9 says, "Honor the Lord with your wealth, with the firstfruits of all your crops." The biblical term *firstfruits* refers to the offerings the Israelites brought to God when they gave Him the earliest fruits of their crops, believing in faith that He would bless them with a great harvest (Exodus 23:16, 19). Obeying God in this way could have been challenging because if they gave away their firstfruits and then, for some reason, the crops didn't yield any more, they would have been left with nothing.

God asks for our firstfruits because giving Him our firsts requires placing our faith in Him. When we give the earliest evidence that our efforts are producing something, we demonstrate our trust in Him, believing that He is faithful and will take our firstfruits as seed and multiply them back to us in an amazing harvest. In God's Kingdom we must lose something in order to gain more (Luke 9:23–25). This principle sounds upside-down from anything we learn in the world, but it works. The Word of God promises us that we will reap what we sow (Galatians 6:7). We also have the testimonies of thousands upon thousands of people who have experienced blessings in response to obeying God's request for our firstfruits, or the first 10 percent (a tithe) of all of our increase.

Some people say that, because tithing was part of the Old Covenant, then under the New Covenant we have with God through Christ, we are no longer required to tithe as a law. But tithing is a biblical principle that honors God and opens the door to many blessings in our lives. As New Testament believers, we are called to be generous and give extravagant freewill offerings, giving joyously, freely, and abundantly. I believe if the Israelites could tithe under the law, we can give even more than 10 percent by grace. The covenant of grace, which Jesus instituted, is better than the covenant of the law (Hebrews 7:22; 8:6), and giving out of desire is certainly better than giving out of duty. Everything we have belongs to God because it all comes from Him. We are not owners of anything, but God trusts us to be good stewards of everything He allows us to enjoy.

If we honor the Lord with our wealth, our barns will be overflowing, meaning that we will have all we need and an abundance to share with others. The Old Testament prophet Malachi writes in regard to tithing that if we will do it, God will open the windows of heaven and pour out blessings so great that we will not have enough room to store them (Malachi 3:10).

If you were to ask me, "Joyce, do you believe we *have* to tithe?" I would say no, because I don't think we can buy God's favor and blessing with our money. God desires generous givers whose hearts are in their giving.

> Each of you should give what you have decided in your heart to give, not reluctantly or under compulsion, for God loves a cheerful giver. And God is able to bless you abundantly, so that in all things at all times, having all that you need, you will abound in every good work.
>
> 2 Corinthians 9:7–8

If you were to ask me if I think it is unwise not to tithe, I would say, "I think it's very unwise to not give God 10 percent at the very least—and anything else He asks for." I don't feel that tithing is an obligation; it is something we do because we love God so much that we want to give generously to Him.

I've heard people say, "I have to pay my tithe," but I don't think that phrase is biblical. We don't pay for anything God gives us, but we do keep in mind that it is more blessed to give than to receive (Acts 20:35). Since I believe this scripture is true, I have no problem with giving all I can give and knowing God will always meet all of my needs (Philippians 4:19).

WISDOM LOVES DISCIPLINE

Proverbs 3:11 mentions discipline, which is not usually a popular topic. For someone to say, "I am simply not a disciplined person" is incorrect, because God has given us a spirit of "discipline and self-control" (2 Timothy 1:7 AMPC). In addition, self-control is a fruit of the Holy Spirit (Galatians 5:22–23). As believers, we have self-control, but people do not always use what they have. The more we use self-restraint or self-control, the stronger it becomes. God tells us the proper way to behave, but He also gives us free will, and He will not force us to do the right thing. Therefore, we need to discipline ourselves to do what we know is right even when we don't want to. We don't have to "feel" like doing the right (godly) thing in order to do it.

If we don't discipline ourselves, then God will discipline us. According to Proverbs 3:11–12, we are not to resent His discipline, but to recognize it as a sign of His great love for us. Many parents who do not discipline their children do not love them. If we think love is giving a child everything they want and letting them do anything they want to do, then we are wrong. That it is a recipe for disaster. I have heard that a large number of people who are in prison say their parents never disciplined them.

THE PROMISES ATTACHED TO WISDOM

Walking in wisdom comes with benefits, and it is "more profitable than silver and yields better returns than gold" (v. 14). Wisdom is also "more precious than rubies," and nothing we desire can compare to the value of wisdom (v. 15). She brings us long life and "riches and honor"; all of her ways are pleasant, and "all her paths are peace" (vv. 16–17). I desire peace more than anything, and it is not easy to maintain in the days in which we live. The apostle James writes that wisdom is "first of all pure; then peace-loving, considerate, submissive, full of mercy and good fruit, impartial and sincere" (James 3:17). We can see from this verse that a wise person will be a maker and maintainer of peace. The benefit for those who make and keep peace is that they will "reap a harvest of righteousness" (James 3:18). Jesus is our wisdom from God (1 Corinthians 1:30), and if we follow His example in how we live, we will experience the benefits of wisdom.

Wise people will not be afraid when they lie down at the end of each day because their sleep will be sweet (v. 24). Just think about what keeps people awake at night. It is usually worry about their problems or about something they have said or done that caused problems for themselves or for others. Had they operated in wisdom, they could have avoided problems altogether. Some people can't sleep for thinking about their debt and the bills they need to pay. Usually, people who lie awake worrying about debt could have avoided it had they used wisdom in handling their money.

> *Can you think of any troublesome areas in your life that could have been avoided if you had followed wisdom?*

Just as ignoring wisdom causes trouble, heeding wisdom brings blessings. The promises that Proverbs makes to those who seek and walk in wisdom, including the promises in chapter 3, are astounding.

DO ALL THE GOOD YOU CAN

Anytime a person is in need and you have the power to meet that need, it is wise to do so. The way to overcome evil is with good (Romans 12:21). One of the best times to do good is when your enemies are attacking you.

When we are under attack, we often withdraw and waste time feeling sorry for ourselves. But we can defeat our enemy, the devil, and whomever he works through by practicing what

I call "the warfare of love." I believe love is a form of spiritual warfare because the enemy wants us to hate one another and be divided. He wants our love to grow cold and dull, but we can keep it active through practicing it daily. Love is seen in how we treat people, and wisdom instructs us not to accuse people without reason when they have done us no harm (v. 30). We need to be merciful toward people and not quick to judge or criticize them. To paraphrase John Wesley, a powerful minister in eighteenth-century England, let me urge you to do as much good as you can, to as many people as you can, as often as you can, and you will experience great joy and many other blessings from God.

PROVERBS 4

The Book of Proverbs is filled with promises for those who choose wisdom, understanding, knowledge, prudence, discretion, discernment, and the fear of the Lord. It is also filled with warnings for those who don't. I have learned that we often ignore warnings that, if heeded, could save us much trouble. For example, many people get sick because they ignore physical symptoms that indicate they are working too hard or are under too much stress. I have been one of those people on more than one occasion.

Consider these warnings: The crew of the *Titanic*, which sank in 1912, ignored warnings, so the ship sank, killing 1,512 people. Cigarette packages warn that smoking is dangerous, but according to the CDC, as of 2018, 34.2 million people in the United States still smoke. Human nature usually assumes we will be the ones who won't have a problem— despite the warnings. That could be true. But it often is not true, and then we pay the price for our unwise choices.

Other disasters that resulted from ignored warnings include the sinking of the *Lusitania* in 1915; the bombing of Pearl Harbor on December 7, 1941; the *Challenger* disaster in 1986; Hurricane Katrina; and Cyclone Nargis, which killed more than one hundred thousand people in Burma in 2008.

Had people heeded the warnings about these tragic events, many lives could have been saved. I'm sure we have all disregarded certain warnings, but going forward we can learn to use wisdom and realize that when God warns us, He is trying to help us avoid future pain and misery.

GIVING UP IN ORDER TO GAIN

Gaining wisdom may be costly (v. 7). However, people who are willing to pay the price will be richly blessed in every area of their lives. In God's economy we often have to give up something we have in order to gain what we truly want, which is consistent with the principle of sowing and reaping. A young person who wants to be a doctor must be willing to sacrifice money and invest several years of study and hard work to gain the education needed to actually become what they want to be. Once they have made the sacrifice, they can enjoy the achievement of their goal and the reality of living what was once a dream. Sacrifice and reward are part of any successful life.

TAKE TIME TO SEEK WISDOM

Life becomes easier when we walk in the seven foundational principles of Proverbs. We are promised that when we walk, our steps will not be hampered, and when we run, we will not stumble (v. 12). Just think about how much time we

waste if we don't take time to seek and heed wisdom. I think
it is safe to say that every divorce is caused by at least one
person in the marriage ignoring godly principles; every bank-
ruptcy and every failed business can be attributed to the same
problem. Wisdom requires that we slow down and take time
to consider and examine situations before we get involved
in them and, once we are involved in them, to thoughtfully
solve problems through wise decision-making.

We frequently make commitments without considering
what fulfilling them will actually require of us. I once asked
a friend in ministry how she decided which speaking invita-
tions to accept and which to decline. She told me that before
she responded to an invitation, she thought through every
detail of what it would take for her to do it. She thought
about matters such as how long she would be away from
home, what kind of preparation time she would need
to invest, and how far would she have to travel. Although
these are all logistical questions and not ministry-related
ones, she was wise to ask them. If we do not ask wise questions, we may agree to do something and then later complain
about it and dread doing it because we did not consider the
details involved in it. It is always better to pray and think
about a commitment before giving an answer.

MAKING PROGRESS

Walking in wisdom and in the other principles found in the
Book of Proverbs is a process that takes time. Just as the sun

shines brighter and brighter as the day progresses (v. 18), so does our godly behavior. Let me encourage you not to be discouraged if you realize you have made many mistakes because you did not use wisdom. Just begin now to search for it with all of your heart. Looking back never helps or improves the future. All we can do about our mistakes is to confess them, ask God to forgive us for them, and then learn from them. Our mistakes can probably educate us more than most other experiences if we will let them.

The apostle John wrote that if we continue in God's Word, we will know the truth and it will make us free (John 8:31–32 KJV). Continuing in God's Word involves more than merely reading or hearing it. It involves meditating on the Scriptures and actually putting them into practice in our lives. Proverbs 4:21–22 teaches us to not let God's words out of our sight and to keep them within our hearts, "for they are life to those who find them and health to one's whole body."

God's Word is very powerful, and it accomplishes great things in and through us if we continue in it. Keeping our heart full of it is one of the wisest things we can do.

Above all else, guard your heart, for everything you do flows from it.

Proverbs 4:23

What we allow into our hearts is very important because it becomes part of us. For this reason, we should make sure that what we allow to come into and remain in our hearts is what we truly want in life. For example, if we allow anger to take root in our hearts, we will experience the unpleasant results of anger in our lives. What is in our hearts will eventually come out in the form of words (Matthew 12:34), and the power of life and death is in the words we speak (Proverbs 18:21). We are to keep our mouths free from perversity and keep "corrupt talk" far from us (v. 24).

As I read Proverbs, it is clear to me that God's will is for us to have and enjoy an amazing life. In His goodness, He has shown us the path we should follow if we want to live that way. However, if we don't follow His wisdom, we forfeit much of what Jesus has provided for us through His death and resurrection. Many people will be in heaven who never enjoyed the lives they lived while they were on their way to eternity.

STAY FOCUSED ON THE GOAL

Many things compete for our attention, but in order to reach our goals we need to practice staying focused on what is most important. We should keep Jesus first above all else, and next we should focus on what He has called us to do. Perhaps God has blessed you with five children to raise, and right now you need to focus on them. Later in life, your focus may need to change because you will be in a different season of your life. Proverbs 4:25–27 puts it like this: "Let your eyes look straight ahead; fix your gaze directly before you. Give careful thought to the paths for your feet and be steadfast in all your ways. Do not turn to the right or the left; keep your foot from evil."

My husband, Dave, recently had a stiff neck and could not turn his head to the right or to the left. I teasingly told him that perhaps God was forcing him to focus on what was in front of him. Focus has become a huge problem for most people these days. Life is filled with distractions from social media, our phones, and our computers—and the demands of daily life have become more complicated than ever.

While I was writing this book, my granddaughter was planning her wedding. Her plans were so much more complicated than the plans Dave and I made when we married more than fifty years ago. The cost of a wedding can be very stressful these days unless a couple has the courage to do things in a simple way. I say that having a simple wedding takes courage because it seems that a variety of people have expectations that can pressure the bride and groom to do things they really don't want to do. I know of one girl whose cousin expected to be a bridesmaid in her wedding. Because the bride didn't ask the cousin to be a bridesmaid, their immediate families didn't speak to one another for more than a year!

> *Do you let the pressure of other people's expectations complicate your life, or do you follow your heart and behave wisely?*

I believe wisdom would have us simplify as much as we possibly can because we gain the benefit of peace when we do so. When our planning or our activities become so complicated that we no longer have peace or cannot enjoy them, I think it is time to step back and reevaluate them.

Writing this book on Proverbs has opened my eyes to just

how important God considers wisdom to be. The theme of the seven key principles is repeated in all thirty-one chapters of the book in some way or another. I urge you to choose wisdom above all else. Teach it to your children and model it in your own life so all who know you may learn from your example of walking in wisdom.

PROVERBS 5

Proverbs 5 is a warning against adultery. This chapter, half of chapter 6, and all of chapter 7 are all about adultery, so it must be a very important subject. Obviously, it is a topic we need to learn more than a little bit about. For some people, sexual lust is an intense desire that demands gratification and becomes one of the strongest temptations they face.

The Bible teaches us not to have sexual intercourse prior to marriage and not to have sex after we are married with anyone other than our spouse (vv. 15–21; Hebrews 13:4; 1 Corinthians 6:15–7:3). The writings of Proverbs make clear that it is very unwise—and sinful—to commit adultery.

Proverbs 5 depicts an unfaithful woman attempting to lure a man into her trap. Both men and women struggle with sexual sin. According to the Institute for Family Studies, 20 percent of men and 13 percent of women have extramarital affairs. Based on this research and other studies, it appears that men are more easily tempted to commit sexual sin than women are. But as we look at what Proverbs has to say about the subject, let's remember that the warnings apply to both men and women.

Adultery is presented as a sin that lures one in through

enticements such as seductive words and suggestive manners of dress (7:5, 10, 21). A seducer is also persistent, but in a sly and cunning way, drawing in the victim gradually (7:10–27).

An adulterous affair begins with little things that may seem harmless when looked at individually. A woman at the office occasionally takes donuts to a man who is her "friend." She compliments him and his work. He needs and values her affirmation, because when he gets home from work at night, his wife is exhausted from dealing with several children and household duties all day. She needs and expects her husband to say and do things to build her confidence, yet she fails to realize that he needs the same from her. Since he is "compliment deficient," when the woman at work compliments him, he cannot help but enjoy the praise and perhaps find himself wanting to see her more often during the workday—simply because she makes him feel good about himself. The temptation to unfaithfulness may then develop to include imaginations and thoughts that are unwise.

Under the Old Covenant, those who committed adultery broke one of God's Ten Commandments (Exodus 20:14; Leviticus 20:10). Doing so was a punishable offense. Jesus goes a step further and says:

> You have heard that it was said, "You shall not commit adultery." But I tell you that anyone who looks at a woman lustfully has already committed adultery with her in his heart.
>
> Matthew 5:27–28

If we find ourselves thinking about what a romantic relationship with someone other than our marriage partner would be like, we should realize that the enemy is trying to set up perfect circumstances for us to ruin our lives. That's exactly what will happen if we keep going in the directions our minds are trying to take us.

The wisest course of action for a person being tempted would be to stay away from the tempter. If that is not possible because of social or work duties, it is critically important to find other effective ways to create barriers between you and the temptation—through accountability with a trusted friend, even making dramatic changes in an employment or social situation. Saving a marriage from ruin is worth whatever extraordinary measures it takes to put space between the person being tempted and the temptation. We must be aggressive against the temptation to do evil. Otherwise, it won't give up, and we will be caught in its trap.

> *Do you aggressively resist temptation?*

IN THE END

According to the writer of Proverbs, the adulterous woman has lips that "drip honey" and speech that is "smoother than oil; but *in the end* she is bitter as gall, sharp as a double-edged sword. Her feet go down to death; her steps lead straight to the grave" (vv. 3–5, emphasis mine). I want to call your attention to three words in verse 4: *in the end*.

Quite often people live as though there is no tomorrow, but tomorrow always comes. In other words, we may behave as though our actions have no consequences, but they do. Eventually we will be faced with having to deal with those consequences. Our actions today will produce either tomorrow's joy or tomorrow's sorrow. It's up to us!

The young man in Proverbs 5 is urged to listen to wisdom and keep far away from the adulterous woman. Don't go near her, "lest you lose your honor to others and your dignity to one who is cruel" (v. 9). If we don't listen to what wisdom says, we read that strangers will feast on our wealth, and our toil will "enrich the house of another" (v. 10).

Verse 11 continues, "At the end of your life you will groan." Notice the words again: *at the end*. The sensual thrill of adultery lasts for a short time, and then the people involved are left with the consequences, which may include anything from a guilty conscience to the destruction of an entire family. If a family falls apart, it is usually the children who are hurt worst. People need to remember what is at stake when they encounter sexual temptation.

Adultery is a sin that can and usually does have long-lasting negative effects. It can be committed in a few minutes, but its results may last a lifetime. Wisdom always thinks about the result of our actions and asks, "Will I be satisfied later with what I choose today?" Wisdom tells us that people guilty of surrendering to seduction or sexual temptation will ultimately say, "How I hated discipline! How my heart spurned correction! I would not obey my teachers or turn my ear to my instructors. And I was soon in serious trouble" (vv. 12–14). They will regret it, but by the time they do, it will be too late.

HOW TO HANDLE TEMPTATION

Understanding temptation and aggressively resisting it with God's help is the only way to stay one step ahead of the enemy. Temptation is a part of life; even Jesus was tempted. The Holy Spirit led Him into the wilderness to be tempted by the devil forty days and nights (Luke 4:1–13). And Hebrews teaches us that Jesus is our high priest because He has been tempted in every way as we are, yet He never sinned (Hebrews 4:15). He was tempted but was able to resist it, and so can we.

When teaching His disciples to pray, Jesus told them to pray that they would not come into temptation (Matthew 6:13). Notice that He did not tell them to pray that they would not *be tempted*, but that they would not *enter into* temptation. I've heard people say, "So-and-so fell into adultery," but that person did not accidentally "fall" into sexual immorality; they chose it, one step at a time. Manipulation and deception are formidable enemies, but wisdom, discretion, discernment, and understanding are greater, and they are quite able to defeat these enemies if we will listen to them.

We have all probably found ourselves reaping an unpleasant harvest in some area of our lives and asking ourselves, "How did I get here?" We may have been so deceived that we didn't recognize the signs pointing us in a negative direction. If we did recognize them, we were not listening to wisdom. We often allow heated emotions to override everything else we know, but we must take responsibility for our sinful actions or we will never be free from them.

The enemy often tries to convince us that we simply cannot resist the temptation to sin. We should never allow him to get away with this, because we definitely can resist temptation. God has promised to never allow more to come on us than what we can bear. With every temptation He will "provide a way out so that you can endure it" (1 Corinthians 10:13).

Don't be afraid you cannot resist temptation, but don't make the mistake of thinking you are so strong that you cannot be tempted. The Bible says that "anyone who thinks he stands [who feels sure that he has a steadfast mind and is standing firm], take heed lest he fall [into sin]" (1 Corinthians 10:12 AMPC). We can do nothing without God (John 15:5), but we can do anything with Him (Philippians 4:13). In our human strength, many things are impossible, "but with God all things are possible" (Matthew 19:26). Always, always, always lean and rely on God because He is your strength, and He enables you to resist sin.

GOD SEES ALL

All of our ways "are in full view of the Lord" (v. 21). God wants us to remember that He sees everything that everyone does. I believe that truly desiring to please our Lord and training ourselves to live in the realization that He sees all will help us avoid wrong actions that end in trouble for us.

Consider and meditate on these scriptures:

Nothing in all creation is hidden from God's sight. Everything is uncovered and laid bare before the eyes of him to whom we must give account.

Hebrews 4:13

The eyes of the Lord are everywhere, keeping watch on the wicked and the good.

Proverbs 15:3

Realizing that God sees everything I do and knows every word in my mouth, even ones I have not yet spoken, is very helpful to me, and I believe it will help you, too (Psalm 139:4).

There is nowhere we can go from the presence of God (Psalm 139:7). We can take great comfort in knowing that He is with us all the time and that He is always ready to help us if we cry out to Him. But we must also recognize that He sees everything we do and hears every word we speak. Perhaps realizing this will help us have the reverential fear and awe of God that is the beginning of wisdom, according to Proverbs 1:7 and 9:10.

> *Do you live your life with an awareness of God's presence?*

LISTEN TO WISDOM'S WHISPER

In studying Proverbs as I prepared to write this book, I began to hear wisdom whisper to me throughout the day, and I continue to hear it. This morning I was trying to decide which of my tops to wear. In my closet, I have a section of casual tops, and I wanted one of those, since I would be home all day. As I pushed hangers back and forth trying to make a decision, I heard the faintest whisper in my heart say, "Any of them will be just fine." We waste a lot of time and add frustration to our lives by being double-minded about things that could be very simple.

Another example occurred yesterday when I overheard part of a conversation about something taking place at our office. I immediately began to go over in my mind all the various scenarios I thought could be happening, and then wisdom whispered, "You don't need to get involved in this." I have turned most of the daily operations of our office over to other capable people, and that means I need to let them do their jobs and trust that they will call on me if and when they need me.

When we get involved in situations we don't need to be involved in, we can quickly lose our peace and our focus. Staying out of situations in which we don't need to be involved keeps our minds at rest and gives us time to focus on our priorities instead of being distracted by other things.

Train yourself to listen to wisdom. Ask God to help you hear it, even when it whispers. The more you pay attention to wisdom, the more you will enjoy your life.

PROVERBS 6

Like many chapters in Proverbs, this one teaches us several important principles. Following them will be pleasing to God and enhance our daily lives.

DON'T COSIGN FOR SOMEONE ELSE'S DEBT

To cosign a loan is to agree to pay a debt if the principal party—the person who takes out the loan and will benefit from it—does not pay it. I wonder how many people have cosigned a loan for someone and then later regretted it because they ended up having to pay the debt when the primary borrower failed to do so.

When a family member or a good friend cannot secure a loan for a car or isn't able to rent an apartment or purchase a home unless they have someone cosign, it is very hard to say no if they ask for our help. However, that is exactly what Proverbs 6:1–5 teaches us to do. There may be exceptions to this, such as having a child who is a young adult and has not had time to establish credit. Often, in that case, no one will rent to that person without a cosigner. But in most cases, cosigning for a loan is not wise. At the very least, we should never become security for another person's debt unless we know we could pay the debt in full if we had to.

I recommend never pledging to pay another person's debts, but if you are going to do it, make sure the person in question doesn't have a history of mismanaging their finances or have difficulty getting and keeping a job. Dave and I once cosigned for my brother and enabled him to rent an apartment because he was trying to put his life back together after years of drug abuse. He had been doing well for two years, held a good job, and was actively involved in various ministry opportunities. But that situation did not end well. He went back to his old ways and left town without even saying goodbye. Dave and I had to work out an agreement with the owner of the property. Thankfully he let us out of the lease, and we only had to pay for the current month.

Proverbs recommends not obligating ourselves to others financially. But if one person has already become security for another person's debts, Solomon says, that one should work "to the point of exhaustion" to be free from the pledge (v. 3). God doesn't want us to carry the stress of making sure other people pay their debts when we have enough to do managing our own finances.

THE SLUGGARD

Proverbs refers to a lazy person as a "sluggard" and recommends that he watch the behavior of the ant to "consider its ways and be wise!" (v. 6). The ant "has no commander, no overseer or ruler, yet it stores its provisions" in times of abundance for times of lack that may come in the future (vv. 7–8). I appreciate these lessons from the ant because they teach me that wise people can do what they should be doing without anyone telling them they need to do it and that they plan ahead during times of plenty for times of lack. As an employer, I love having employees who are self-motivated and able to do the jobs we have hired them to do without someone standing over them, making sure they do their work.

The Word of God has much to say about lazy people. It teaches us to do whatever we do with all of our heart (Colossians 3:23). This means doing the best job we can possibly do and doing it with zeal and enthusiasm. We are to not only provide for our own families, but also for extended family members who are unable to provide for themselves through circumstances that are not their fault. Children are to take care of their parents and grandparents if they need care, and anyone who doesn't fulfill this responsibility is worse than an unbeliever (1 Timothy 5:8).

In Genesis 2:15, we read that God created man and put him in the Garden of Eden to work and tend it. He didn't put him there to rest under a tree all day while snacking on fruit. Anyone who is lazy or passive can expect to also experience poverty and all the misery that goes with it.

Proverbs teaches us to be prudent, which means we are to be good managers of all our resources, including our time and our energy. Overworking is not healthy, while underworking is laziness and never leads to anything good. God wants us to work and to take time to enjoy the blessings our work yields. The longer a person is lazy, the lazier he or she becomes.

The only cure for laziness is action. At first, rousing oneself from laziness may be difficult, but a little discipline and diligence to do so will pay off in the end. Here is a saying that I heard and really like: "The more you move, the more you can move; the less you move, the less you can move." This is why it is important for elderly people to keep moving. They will live longer and be more energetic if they do.

> Do you maintain a good balance between work and rest?

Solomon instructs the lazy man not to lie around napping and not doing much of anything, because it will cause poverty to come on him "like a thief and scarcity like an armed man" (v. 11). Sometimes you will need to sow hard work for what seems like a long time before you start to see its benefits. During that time you may feel tempted to give up or do the minimum required, but I urge you to keep being vigilant and working hard because it will bring a wonderful harvest of many good things.

DON'T BE A TROUBLEMAKER

Some people do all kinds of things that could cause them to be known as troublemakers. Gossip, tale bearing, and starting or feeding strife at work, at home, or in the church are some of them. I like the definition of strife that refers to it as an "angry undercurrent." Most of the time, strife is not out in the open; it is more often a quiet, underground movement of disgruntled people who talk to one another about all they are not happy with but never deal directly with the person with whom they are unhappy. We should not stir up strife, feed it, or keep fanning its flames by adding to it.

Jesus says that if we have anything against our brother or sister, we should go to that person privately and try to settle the matter. If that doesn't work, we should take two or three others with us. If all else fails, we are to go to the church with our complaint (Matthew 18:15–17). It is sad to think about how often we talk to people who have no ability to solve our problem and never go to the one person with whom we might work to find a solution.

A troublemaker—a villain—is said to be someone with a "corrupt mouth" (v. 12). This person "plots evil with deceit in his heart" (v. 14) and is cunning, malicious, and conniving. There is no way such a person will come to a pleasant end. In fact, "disaster will overtake him in an instant; he will suddenly be destroyed—without remedy" (v. 15).

Troublemakers may think they are getting away with what they are doing, but they are sowing bad seed that will produce destruction for them in due time. The message wisdom wants us to learn in Proverbs is this: Do the right thing now, and you will love the results later.

> *When you are having a problem with someone, do you go to that person privately to discuss it, or do you go to others and talk about the one who has offended you?*

SIX THINGS THE LORD HATES

According to Proverbs 6:16–19, there are "six things the Lord hates, seven that are detestable to him: haughty eyes, a lying tongue, hands that shed innocent blood, a heart that devises wicked schemes, feet that are quick to rush into evil, a false witness who pours out lies and a person who stirs up conflict in the community." Let's consider each one.

Haughty Eyes

The first thing the Lord hates is haughty eyes, meaning a person so filled with pride that their arrogance can be seen in the way they look at other people. They can give people the "You are stupid" look, or the "I know more than you do" look. People can actually say more through facial expressions and body language than with words. God wants us to know that anything we can do is because of His goodness and grace, not our own abilities. And Paul writes that we should not ever think of ourselves more highly than we should (Romans 12:3), which is exactly what haughtiness is.

I like to say that Jesus is the great equalizer. His promises are for everyone who will obey Him, regardless of race, education, social standing, accomplishment, or gender. We are all one in Him. None of us is anything without Him, but all of us can do anything He wants us to do through Him (Philippians 4:13). No one is better than anyone else, but no one is less than anyone else, either. Therefore, no one has any reason to be haughty.

A Lying Tongue

A lying tongue is something else the Lord hates. Jesus says that He is the truth (John 14:6), His Word is truth (John 17:17), and the truth will make us free (John 8:32). No wonder He hates lying (untruth). Many people will say whatever they need to say in order to get what they want, and they will lie to stay out of trouble if they have done something wrong. But a person committed to truth will tell the truth even if it causes personal loss or pain.

Hands That Shed Innocent Blood

The Lord also hates hands that shed innocent blood. This would certainly apply to committing murder, but I think it also takes into account anyone who mistreats another person. God especially hates it if we oppress those who are helpless, such as widows, orphans, the poor, and the ill or infirm. Not taking action to help people who need assistance is equivalent to mistreatment. If we have the ability to help another person and simply choose not to do so, God does not like our lack of action. We often pray for God to do something to help people in need when we could easily help them ourselves, but just don't want to.

A group of ministers were praying and asking God to provide the funds needed to cover the convention they were having. Suddenly one minister stopped the prayer and said, "There's no need to pray about that. We can easily cover the cost between all of us." They were able to meet the need themselves; they simply needed to realize that they had the ability to do it.

A Heart That Devises Wicked Schemes

God hates a heart that devises wicked schemes, which describes a person whose mind is filled with selfish ideas of how they can profit without working or how they can cause trouble for someone they are jealous of or exact revenge on someone who has hurt them. God wants our minds to be filled with His thoughts—positive, lovely thoughts that plan good things for other people and think of ways to bless them. Whatever is in our minds leads to our actions, or as I often say, "Where the mind goes, the man follows." God's Word says to think about these things: "Whatever is true, whatever is noble, whatever is right, whatever is pure, whatever is lovely, whatever is admirable" (Philippians 4:8). As we fix our minds on them, the Scripture promises that "the God of peace will be with you" (Philippians 4:9).

Feet That Are Quick to Rush into Evil

Another thing God hates are feet that are quick to rush into evil, meaning an eagerness to cause mischief, create problems, or hurt people. Let me be clear that God doesn't hate people who do these things, but He does hate their evil actions. He hates them not only because they are evil but also because He knows they will cause trouble for those who do them. God is good, and He only wants good for His children, so of course He is grieved and displeased when we do things that He knows will harm us. We all feel that way about our children, and God is the ultimate parent, so naturally He would feel that way, too.

Notice the phrase "feet that are *quick to rush* into evil" (emphasis mine). I am learning after a lifetime of doing things wrong and seeing the consequences—and of doing things right and seeing the consequences—that rushing usually causes a problem of some kind. Rushing causes us to miss what wisdom is trying to tell us. Decisions made hastily or words spoken rashly almost always bring regret. I am striving to live an unhurried life, but I find it more difficult than I might have thought. I am slowly making progress, but this is one of those times I wish God would hurry up and teach me not to rush, if you know what I mean. It's kind of funny when you really think about it: God is trying to teach us not to hurry, and we are usually trying to get Him to hurry!

I wonder how many people are in prison because they rushed into something without giving any thought to the potential consequences of their actions. Each of our actions causes a reaction, so nothing should be done in such a hurry that we have no time to think about what we are doing and how it will affect us and others.

A False Witness Who Pours Out Lies

The sixth thing the Lord hates pertains to lying, which Solomon has already mentioned in this list. The fact that he repeats it means we should pay close attention to it. When a false witness tells lies, they are the type of lies that get someone else in trouble. A false witness may say he saw someone

Do you always tell the truth no matter what?

do something wrong or heard that someone committed a crime, but either he did not see or hear it, or he lies about what he did witness or hear. We have already read that God hates a lying tongue, and it seems as if He is elaborating on it to make sure we don't miss it.

A Person Who Stirs Up Conflict (Strife) in the Community

One thing that is detestable to the Lord is a person who stirs up conflict, or strife, in the community. I have explained strife and its dangers, but it is interesting that strife is something the Lord seems to particularly detest. Strife is like a cancer. It eats away at the peace of a group of people, stirs up trouble, and little by little destroys the group.

I was once part of a church that no longer exists because of strife. The pastors tried to exercise too much control over the congregation, and the people murmured and complained about them behind the scenes. Strife destroys the anointing of the Holy Spirit, but unity brings blessings (Psalm 133: 1–3). Once again, I urge you not to participate in strife and do all you can to stop it if you know it exists in your group.

A FURTHER WARNING AGAINST ADULTERY

Proverbs 6:20–35 warns again about the dangers of adultery. Verse 32 says that the one who commits adultery has "no sense" and is destroying himself. No one can commit adultery without suffering afterward for that sin. It is not possible! This section of Proverbs states this very clearly. It says, "Can a man walk on hot coals without his feet being scorched? So is he who sleeps with another man's wife; no one who touches her will go unpunished" (vv. 28–29). These ominous warnings should help us say no to sexual temptation so we can avoid the misery it obviously causes. Be wise and do now what you will be happy with later.

PROVERBS 7

Before warning once again about adultery, Proverbs 7:1–3 says:

> "My son, keep my words and store up my commands within you. Keep my commands and you will live; guard my teachings as the apple of your eye. Bind them on your fingers; write them on the tablet of your heart."

Proverbs 7:1–3 reminds me of Psalm 119:11: "I have hidden your word in my heart that I might not sin against you." In Proverbs, Solomon is speaking to his son, and in Psalm 119:11, David is speaking to God. Both scriptures teach us how valuable it is not to simply read truth, but to hide it—or keep it alive—in our hearts. If something is written on the tablet of our hearts, we can see it easily and look at it often. That's the way we are to treat God's Word, as something so dear to us that it is as close as our own hearts.

In his commentary on this section of Proverbs 7, Matthew Henry writes that Solomon "speaks in God's name; for it is God's commandments that we are to keep, his words, his law." He goes on to say that we are to keep God's Word "as our treasure" and that we must lay up (meaning to store in our hearts) God's commandments "that we may not be robbed of them by the wicked one." Reading, studying, and knowing God's Word is vital to us, but it is also vital that we guard His Word as "the apple" of our eye, as Solomon writes, meaning that we protect it and treat it as very precious to us.

Proverbs 7:4 says, "Say to wisdom, 'You are my sister,' and to insight, 'You are my relative.'" This teaches us to love and have a close relationship with wisdom and to consult it often and freely, just as we would speak openly with a family member.

I like the fact that Solomon begins this chapter with an exhortation to value wisdom, because it provides context for his warning against adultery. Instead of simply saying, "Don't commit adultery!" or saying, "Adultery is wrong!" he helps his son understand that avoiding adultery is not only a righteous way to live but also wise. People who walk in wisdom choose righteousness over sin because they love God, honor His Word, and prefer the blessings of wisdom to the consequences of sin.

WISE COUNSEL REGARDING ADULTERY

Proverbs 7 warns once again against adultery. We may assume from how much Solomon writes about adultery that he had firsthand knowledge of the trouble it causes. As a matter of fact, we know that his lustful desire for women led to his downfall.

> King Solomon, however, loved many foreign women besides Pharaoh's daughter—Moabites, Ammonites, Edomites, Sidonians and Hittites. They were from nations about which the Lord had told the Israelites, "You must not intermarry with them, because they will surely turn your hearts after their gods." Nevertheless, Solomon held fast to them in love. He had seven hundred wives of royal birth and three hundred concubines, and his wives led him astray.
>
> 1 Kings 11:1–3

It is no wonder that Solomon warns repeatedly of the dangers of adultery. Much of Proverbs seems to be written from a father to a son, which may be one reason that it warns about staying away from adulterous women without mentioning that men can also be the culprits. As I mentioned in chapter 5, we cannot blame women for all sexual sin. I am sure that women were a great temptation to Solomon, one he was not always able to resist. He instructs his reader to stay away from the path of the adulterous woman, and I am sure he wished many times that he had done so. Even in a culture that practiced polygamy, Solomon's seven hundred wives and three hundred concubines seems excessive. This shows us what a grip lust can have on a person.

AN AGE-OLD PROBLEM

Sexual immorality is not something that God has ever approved of, and it has caused problems for centuries. He stated at the beginning of the world that a man should leave his father and mother and cleave (be united) to his wife (Genesis 2:24). However, after Adam and Eve sinned, the lines of morality blurred. Lamech, a descendant of Adam's son, Cain, had two wives (Genesis 4:19). Polygamy is and always has been wrong. Solomon, David, and the Israelites in general paid steep prices in their relationships with God because they practiced polygamy and many other forbidden behaviors. However, God still loved them and kept taking them back anytime they repented and returned to Him.

To help the people of Israel understand their spiritual adultery, God told the prophet Hosea to marry a prostitute (Hosea 1:2). Hosea's love for his unfaithful wife was a picture of God's heart for His people and showed them how He would deal with them (Hosea 3:1–5; 14:1–9). I am sure Hosea hoped his wife would turn from her former passions and love only him, but she went back to her previous ways and loved another man. God told Hosea to take her back again and love her as He loved the Israelites, though they turned to other gods (Hosea 3:1). Studying the entire Book of Hosea is eye-opening concerning God's unconditional love for and mercy not only toward Israel but for all who sin.

God had instructed the Israelites to keep Him first and

have no other gods (Exodus 20:3), yet they intermarried with other nations and worshipped their gods (Jeremiah 44: 15–17). They belonged to God, but they behaved as though they belonged to the world. He said they had prostituted themselves (Jeremiah 5:7–8). Hosea's story shows us clearly how amazing God's unconditional love is. Thank God for His great mercy and forgiveness toward repentant sinners!

The problem of turning away from God was not unique to Old Testament times, nor is it unique to our day. It was common in the early church as well. In James's letter to the church, he writes under the inspiration of the Holy Spirit that the people were "adulterous people" because they had made friendships with the world that caused them to act against God's will (James 4:4).

We belong to God, not to ourselves (1 Corinthians 6:19–20). He gives us free will and wants us to use that ability to choose to serve Him and to follow His will for our lives. He gives us the power to choose because He does not desire for us to love Him because we feel forced to do so. The strength and beauty of love is that we *choose* to feel and express it. His will is for us to keep Him first in all things at all times and to obey Him because we trust and love Him. He purchased us with the blood of His Son, Jesus. Truly we are not our own, but we often behave as though we are. We are at liberty to choose our path. But God's Word tells us plainly that choosing the narrow path (God's will) leads to life in all of its fullness and that the broad path (not God's will) leads to destruction (Matthew 7:13–14).

FAITHFULNESS

Proverbs 7:6–27 is about a young man's interaction with a harlot, and it helps us see clearly the consequences of unfaithful living. People who walk in wisdom are faithful to God, and they reap the benefits of that faithfulness.

God Himself is faithful. We love to hear about and sing about the faithfulness of God. However, just as He is faithful to us, He expects us to be faithful to Him and faithful in all of our ways and dealings with people. Certainly, faithfulness is expected in marriage, and adultery is the opposite of faithfulness. To be faithful means to be loyal, devoted, true, constant, stable, dependable, and devoted. When a man and a woman marry and pledge to be faithful to one another, they each promise to be true to that one person in every way, and sexual faithfulness is one of the most important aspects of a good marriage. Sexual sin can be forgiven, but it damages a relationship in such a way that it is rarely completely repaired. A lack of faithfulness creates trust issues, and regaining lost trust usually takes a long time and lots of hard work.

GOD PROMOTES FAITHFUL
MEN AND WOMEN

The Bible says that Moses was faithful in all the household of God (Numbers 12:7). He led the Israelites through the wilderness for forty years. That is 14,600 days, according to our

modern calendar! They murmured and complained, were
impatient, and frequently blamed Moses and God for their
problems instead of taking responsibility for themselves. To
say that Moses was powerful would almost seem an under-
statement. God used him to bring down ten different plagues
on Egypt, to part the Red Sea, and to do many other miracles
(Exodus 4:1–12:30; 14:21–22). Moses was the one chosen
to go to the top of Mount Sinai and receive the Ten Commandments (Exodus 20:1–17). Others went part of the way
with him, but they were only allowed to go so far. Surely, his
faithfulness was part of the reason God used him as He did.

In contrast, a young man named Samson, who is also
mentioned in the Old Testament, was "dedicated to God from
the womb" (Judges 13:5). Because of that, we might expect
that he would have remained faithful to the Lord for his entire
life. But as you may know, that's not how his story unfolds.

Samson had tremendous physical strength (Judges 14:5–
6; 15:14–16), but he did not have the spiritual strength to
stand up to the temptation he faced with a beautiful woman
named Delilah. She tempted him, and as a result, he broke
his covenant with God. He told her the secret to the power
God had given him and as a result, he lost his power completely (Judges 16:4–21).

Like Samson, we may start out with the best intentions,
determined to be faithful in all our ways. That commitment
may last for quite a long time, but what happens when we
begin to grow weary? The apostle Paul dealt with weariness
and writes that we are not to be "weary in doing good, for at
the proper time we will reap a harvest if we do not give up"

(Galatians 6:9). I often say that it is not what we do right one time that brings God's reward into our lives, but it is what we do right over and over and over again. Giving up is easy, but faithfulness is required to remain committed to something even after the excitement of it wanes. New experiences and endeavors often carry with them emotional enthusiasm, but what will we do after the initial excitement subsides and we are left with a duty that has not yet brought the reward we desire? These times when excitement fizzles out and we must live according to our commitments are the times when faithful men and women keep going even after others give up.

Self-discipline is required if we intend to be faithful, because there will be times when we want to quit or stray from our original commitments. Discipline usually hurts before it brings reward, but the reward always comes in due time if we do not give up. God is a "rewarder of those who diligently seek Him" (Hebrews 11:6 NKJV), and diligence always brings benefits.

Even though we find in Proverbs 7 that young men are frequently tempted to commit adultery, we also find wisdom calling out, promising to protect and direct them if they will heed it (Proverbs 8:1–4). God has an answer to all of our

> *Do you make a priority of keeping your commitments?*

temptations and problems, and when we call on Him, He will always give us the strength to endure any temptation that comes. When we realize we are being tempted, we should flee for our very lives. Sin is persuasive and seduces with "smooth talk," but anyone who follows it will become "like an ox going to the slaughter," or "a bird darting into a snare, little knowing it will cost him his life" (vv. 21–23).

You might feel that you have wasted many years and sincerely wish you had heeded wisdom before you experienced the pain of not listening to it. However, it is never too late to begin. Every wise decision you make helps override an unwise one you may have made in the past. Follow wisdom and rejoice in your victories!

PROVERBS 8

Proverbs 8 begins with wisdom's reminder that she is always calling out to us (v. 1) and there is great reward in listening to her. The words of wisdom are always trustworthy, and everything she speaks is right and true. The Lord brought wisdom forth as His first work before He did anything else centuries ago (Proverbs 8:6–7, 22).

I remain intrigued by how frequently the seven foundational principles we see in Proverbs 1 are repeated throughout the thirty-one chapters of Proverbs. This tells me how important they are and that we need to be reminded of them often so we will not drift away from them. Most of those principles are mentioned in Proverbs 8. It says that *understanding* raises her voice (v. 1), and those who are simple should gain *prudence* (v. 5). To those who are *discerning,* all the instructions of *wisdom* are right (v. 9). They are upright to those who have *knowledge* (v. 9). Wisdom says that she dwells with *prudence* (good management) and possesses *knowledge* and *discretion* (v. 12). As I mentioned in the introduction to this book, one characteristic that stands out to me about these wonderful traits is that having them requires patience and a willingness to wait on God.

Proverbs 8 also reminds us that those who walk in the

fear of the Lord hate evil (v. 13). I believe that when we have a proper fear of the Lord we hate what He hates. We hate to see people treated unjustly, abused, or belittled. Instead, we work for justice. An example of this would be the human trafficking tragedy so prevalent today. Most people think it is terrible, but how many do anything about it? You might ask, "What can I do?" You can pray, and financially support ministries that are actively working to free human trafficking victims. To merely feel bad about something that is unjust does nothing to fix it. Only proper action brings solutions. God works through people, so we should offer ourselves as vessels for Him to work through in overcoming evil of all kinds. We also hate to see people ruining their lives through doing evil things, and we pray for them and try to teach them truth if they will receive it.

In addition, wisdom informs us that she was formed long ago "at the very beginning, when the world came to be" (v. 23). God prepared everything we would need to live a wonderful life before He created us. Wisdom says that she was "constantly" at God's side while He was creating the world (v. 30). She delighted "day after day," rejoicing in the presence of God, rejoicing over His creation, and "delighting in mankind" (vv. 30–31).

Wisdom sees the possibilities of the blessed lives people could enjoy and says:

> Listen to my instruction and be wise; do not disregard it. Blessed are those who listen to me, watching daily at my doors, waiting at my doorway. For those who find

me find life and receive favor from the Lord. But those who fail to find me harm themselves; all who hate me love death.

Proverbs 8:33–36

SLOW DOWN

Note that Proverbs 8:34 teaches us to watch and wait at the doorway to wisdom, and we will be blessed. Perhaps one reason we see so little wisdom and so much foolishness in the world today is that most people are in a huge hurry, running from activity to activity without even knowing why they are doing it. *Hurry up* is a frequently used phrase. I heard myself recently say to a guest in my home, "I'm going to hurry up and go to the bathroom, and I'll be right back." There was no need to rush at all, but I guess I felt I had to hurry so I could quickly return to my guest, who happened to be a good friend and had others to talk to in my absence. You might want to pay attention to how often you feel the need to hurry when there is truly no reason to move quickly.

Dave's mother raised six children alone because his father died young. In addition to taking care of the children, she cleaned homes for other people to provide an income for her family. During those years, she had so much to do that she hurried all the time. But when she was older and had no need to hurry, I noticed that she still rushed around doing whatever she was doing.

Rushing can become a habit, and like all bad habits, it can be broken with God's help and determination. To slow down the pace of your life, practice walking slower as you go about each day. Spend longer thinking and praying before making commitments. Take time to breathe and relax between chores. People often say that they are living in the fast lane of life, as though they are proud of it, but in the end, such a rapid pace proves not to be wise.

I work out three mornings each week, and my goal after each workout is to take a shower and get cleaned up for the day. But I have found it really helps me to take five minutes and just sit in my recliner after working out before heading to the shower. I call these moments my "five- minute vacations." To give yourself a break from rushing through each day, you might want to take five-minute vacations, too.

If you feel hurried most of the time, you might start asking yourself why that is the case. You may discover that there is no real reason to rush so much. Perhaps, like Dave's mother, it is simply a habit you have maintained, even though you no longer need to do it. I promise that slowing down will enable you to listen to wisdom more closely. Rushing is hard on the physical body, and it contributes to many different physical ailments. It also causes stress. I can't imagine Jesus hurrying as He went from one activity to the next and from town to town, yet He accomplished more in His three-year ministry than most of us do in a lifetime.

You and I make decisions every day. Some are minor, and others may be major decisions that can have life-altering effects. Each day I choose an outfit to wear, and that is not

a decision that matters much
on most occasions. However,
whether or not to buy a new
car is a more serious decision.
When you face a big decision,

> *Do you hurry too much
> and rush from one thing
> to another?*

take time to really think about it and make sure wisdom and
prudence are leading you, not merely emotions or fleshly
desires.

I'm sure that you, like me, can think of many decisions
that you have made too quickly and have caused turmoil
and perhaps years of trouble. We cannot go back and remake
those choices, but we can learn from our mistakes and go
forward, letting wisdom take the lead.

WHAT ARE THE BENEFITS?

When people are considering whether or not to go to work
for a company, they usually want to know what the benefits
are. They are interested in how much vacation they will have,
whether the employer has a retirement plan, and what kind
of insurance coverage the company provides. These benefits
are as important to many people as their salaries or wages. I
think we all want to know that we will reap benefits from the
effort we put into something, and rightly so.

Wisdom reminds us throughout Proverbs that listening
to her and following her advice will bring amazing benefits.
Several of those benefits are listed in Proverbs 8. For example,
good rulers (leaders) reign by wisdom and they rule justly

(v. 15). In other words, they are fair to everyone. Riches, honor, enduring wealth, and prosperity come with wisdom (v. 18). Why? Because wisdom is prudent; it manages resources in such a way that they can increase and not be lost in foolish or wasteful ways.

I know a man whose parents taught him always to save 10 percent of all his earnings, starting with his allowance when he was a young boy. Because he was wise enough to follow his parents' wisdom, he had enough money saved to buy a home and pay cash for it by the time he married. For years, he resisted spending all of his money on temporary pleasures as soon as he got it, and he was building blessings for his future. He also invested some of his money, so he earned interest on that, causing his money to increase more and more over the years. He did at a young age what would make him happy and satisfied in the future.

His friends, who spent all their money as soon as they received it, often wanted to borrow from him, and he repeatedly had the wisdom to say no. They were like the five foolish virgins in Matthew 25:1–13, who had no extra oil for their lamps while they waited for the bridegroom to come. Because he lingered, they ran out of oil and asked the five wise virgins who had extra oil for some of theirs. The wise virgins told the foolish virgins no. Each of us needs to do what is right, and when we do, we will have right results. But it is not right for people who are lazy or lack wisdom to live off of the hard work of those who have been diligent.

Sometimes we don't want to tell our friends or relatives no, but we should not enable them to continue their unwise lifestyle. By all means, help those who have done their best and find themselves in difficult times, but don't feel that you have to say yes to everyone who asks you for a favor, especially when helping them enables them to continue in a lazy lifestyle.

Dave has been and is a very patient man. He can discipline himself now for a future benefit. When he was a boy, he worked hard cutting people's grass, setting pins at the bowling alley before that function was mechanized, selling papers on the street corner even in freezing weather, and at many other jobs. He gave a large portion of his earnings to his mother to help with the family expenses, but he always saved some. He actually hid money in his socks and put them in the back of his dresser drawer. He paid cash for his first car, bought the family's first television set, and provided other things for himself and others. Because of his ability to be patient and save, our ministry has never been in debt. He always saves first and then pays cash. By doing so, he saves untold amounts of money by not paying interest on loans. We have had to wait for many things, but the wisdom Dave uses has definitely brought us benefits in many ways.

Debt is very oppressive, and wisdom encourages us to owe no one anything but love (Romans 13:8). No one wants to know their paycheck has gone to pay for things they already have before they even get paid. In our society today, most people live on credit. Some may not think there is any other way to live, but wisdom teaches us that there is.

There are occasions when you may have no choice but to borrow money. In that situation, ask yourself before you do it if the item you are borrowing money to have is something you truly need right away. If you are in debt, don't feel guilty, because that won't do any good. But start working toward getting out of debt and staying out. Believe that financial freedom is possible and go for it. You will have to learn to wait on purchases and perhaps even do without some things, but your stress level will decrease and your joy will increase. If you are in deep debt, it may seem overwhelming, as though you can never dig your way out of it. But with persistent diligence, you can. Dave Ramsey does wonderful teaching on how to get out of debt, so I recommend that you check out his material if debt is a problem you need to overcome.

Wisdom says that she bestows a rich inheritance on those who love her, and she makes their treasuries full (v. 21). It is God's will for you to have your needs met and be able to help others out of your overflow, but to do so, you will need to cooperate with Him by following His guidelines on prudence.

PROVERBS 9

Both wisdom and folly cry out to us on a regular basis, and we have to decide which one to follow. In Proverbs 9, we learn that wisdom builds her house (v. 1); she values the home as part of the foundation needed for the rest of life. If things are not right at home, they won't be right anywhere else. Far too many people ignore their families in the quest to build a business, excel in a sport, or achieve a worldly type of success. But God and the home should always come first. What good would it do if I were ministering to others while my family was falling apart at home? Many homes are filled with strife, and the family members who live there are passive about dealing with problems while going out into the world every day and putting on a happy face for others. If we want to live in wisdom, we must make sure our priorities are in order, which requires regular examination of our lives and relationships and making changes where necessary.

People frequently ask me how I keep my priorities straight with all the things I am doing, and my answer is, "I am always straightening them out." I don't think any of us can maintain right priorities without occasionally making adjustments. For example, something may have been a high priority at one time in our lives but is no longer necessary. If we continue doing things that God is finished with, we feel the strain of laboring alone because God only helps us with things that are within His will for us.

> Do you think there may be some things in your life that God is finished with but you are still trying to keep alive?

I encourage you to take some time before the Lord and ask Him to show you any areas in your private life that need attention. Remember, wisdom builds her house before turning her focus to other matters.

TEACH THOSE WHO WANT TO LEARN

Proverbs 9:7–9 says that people will not learn anything unless they are humble enough to receive correction. As I study the Bible I notice that Jesus didn't beg people to let Him help them, but He always helped those who came to Him wanting help. Sometimes we want to help people make positive changes in their lives more than they want to make them. In such cases, we waste valuable energy that could be used elsewhere in a profitable way.

I spent four years trying to help my brother, who was addicted to drugs. Although he appeared to want help, he wasn't willing to do anything that required much effort on his part. I finally realized that if we spend four years trying to help someone and that person still is not helped, then they probably don't really want help. They simply want to be rescued. We can rescue people, but unless they learn to do what is right when they are on their own and making their own decisions, they will only get into trouble again and need another rescue.

Similarly, if we try to correct mockers or the wicked (the ungodly, those who do not live according to God's Word), they will respond with hatred (v. 8). A mocker is someone who displays contempt for what is being taught. Those who mock think they know all they need to know and have no interest in learning. It is impossible to teach people who believe they do not need to learn anything. In contrast, if we correct wise people, according to Proverbs 9:8–9, they will love us, become wiser, and add to their learning.

When I am unable to help someone who clearly needs help, I have learned to pray that God will send into that individual's path the perfect person who can speak a timely, godly word to him or her. As we keep praying, God will keep working with the person for whom we pray.

KNOWLEDGE OF THE HOLY ONE

"The fear of the Lord is the beginning of wisdom, and knowledge of the Holy One is understanding" (v. 10). I want to focus on the word *knowledge* here, because the type of knowledge Solomon writes about goes beyond mere intellectual knowledge. The apostle Paul wrote that his determined purpose in life was to know God and the "power of his resurrection" (Philippians 3:10). Paul already knew God, but he wanted to know Him more deeply and personally. He didn't want to know *about* Him, he wanted to *know* Him. Knowing that God exists barely scratches the surface of what God wants us to know about Him. He wants us to know His character, and that can only be learned through what the Bible refers to as "costly experience" (Proverbs 5:1 AMPC). How can we ever truly know that God is faithful and trustworthy unless we step out in faith and trust Him with situations in our lives? How can we know His mercy if we never ask for and receive it? To truly know anything or anyone, we must have experience with them. Many people might say that they know you, but they don't know you as your family knows you, because your family has experience no one else has had with you.

The knowledge of God is eternal life (John 17:3). Eternal life begins the day we receive Christ as our Savior and Lord, not when we die. The eternal (forever) life God wants us to live is one of righteousness, peace, joy, and abundance in every area. When we speak of abundance or prosperity, we are not speaking merely of money or material goods. More importantly, we are speaking of spiritual prosperity, which is knowing God and experiencing His presence in our daily lives. It is knowing His Word and obeying it. Consider this passage:

> We know that we have come to know him if we keep his commands. Whoever says, "I know him," but does not do what he commands is a liar, and the truth is not in that person. But if anyone obeys his word, love for God is truly made complete in them. This is how we

know we are in him: Whoever claims to live in him
must live as Jesus did.

1 John 2:3–6

Obeying God's commands is what gives us the costly
experience of truly following Him. Even though doing what
God commands is always good for us, it isn't necessarily
always easy. The apostle James said that if we are hearers and
not doers of the Word, we deceive ourselves "by reasoning
contrary to the Truth" (James 1:22 AMPC).

On one occasion, Jesus washed His disciples' feet. At that
time, He told them that He did it as an example so they could
do likewise. He said, "Now that you know these things, you
will be blessed if you do them" (John 13:17). It is important to understand that God's blessing does not come because
we know what He said or did, but it comes when we follow the example He set for us and do as He did. This is one
way we obtain "knowledge of the Holy One" (v. 10).

I have found that it helps me know Jesus better if I really
pay attention to what He is doing in my life and in the lives of
others. God answers so many prayers for us, and sometimes
we fail to recognize or to say thank you for His responses.

Let me encourage you today to take some time and think
about what God has done in your life—in the past week, the
past month, the past year, the past five years. Try keeping a
journal of remembrance—a book in which you write down
the things God gives to you and does for you, along with
the prayers you see Him answer. You can then go back and
remember His greatness, which will strengthen your faith for

the things you are currently dealing with. Remembrance is important. In fact, not remembering the great and mighty acts of God was the Israelites' biggest problem (Judges 8:34). Moses told the Israelites that God wanted them to be careful not to forget all He had done for them once they were living in and enjoying the blessings He provided (Deuteronomy 8:10–11), and they did it anyway.

It is amazing—and sad—to realize how quickly we can return to complaining even after God has blessed us in powerful ways.

THE DANGERS OF FOLLY

Proverbs 9 not only deals with the blessings of wisdom; it also addresses the problems created by folly, which means foolishness. It is foolish to disobey God, and anyone who has the reverential fear and awe of God—who truly knows Him in a deep and intimate way—realizes that. Why would we do foolish things if we truly believe they will bring trouble into our lives? People act foolishly because they think they can do the wrong thing and somehow still get the right result. But I remind you: God's Word lets us know that we reap according to what we have sown (Galatians 6:7).

I believe foolishness calls out to us, just as wisdom does. Foolishness says, "Take the easy road! Do what you feel like doing. Have fun and don't worry about the future. Live for instant gratification. Don't wait to amuse yourself—do it now!" Proverbs indicates that people living this way have "no sense" (v. 16). Little do they know that they are damaging their future and that the price of instant gratification ultimately won't be worth paying.

To me, the Bible has one main message: When we do what God tells us to do, we will be blessed; when we disobey Him, we have troubles heaped on top of troubles. Experience with God teaches us that this is true—and gaining this experience is often costly. Sometimes only the consequences of having done the wrong thing can teach us to do the right thing. Learning to obey God may be a painful lesson at times, but it can save us a great deal of trouble in the future.

Let me give you a practical example from my life. I have been sitting in a recliner for several hours working on this book. More than one doctor, one of whom is a back surgeon who performed a minor surgery on a disc in my back several years ago, have advised me that when I am writing, I should be sure to stand, stretch, walk around the house, and get a little exercise at least once every hour. Well, when I am writing I am focused on the message I want to communicate, and I'm in a flow. The last thing I want to do is stop. However, I can feel when I am getting tired, and I know that is a signal to get up. About fifteen minutes ago, I had one of those times, and although I did not want to, I got up and put on my tennis shoes and went downstairs and walked on my treadmill for fifteen minutes and stretched my back before and after I did it. I took a little break, and now I have returned to work.

I cannot tell you how many years I ignored the feeling of being tired and stiff, and I allowed it to get to the point of exhaustion. Doing so was partially the cause of my back problems and some other physical problems as well. Thankfully, God is gracious to heal us even when we have been foolish, but we often have to go through discomfort we could have avoided had we listened to Him.

> *Can you think of something you had to learn the hard way, through the experience of doing it wrong and reaping the result, before you were willing to do it right?*

Hopefully and prayerfully you will be encouraged to use wisdom and avoid folly, realizing that one brings blessing and the other brings trouble.

PROVERBS 10

Proverbs 10 covers several subjects, but three that stand out to me are the dangers of laziness, the importance of having integrity, and the power of our words. Wisdom understands the impact each of these has on our daily lives. The wise person avoids laziness, walks with integrity, and is careful concerning their words. Wisdom does not live with the misery of regret, because it chooses to take the godly action at the proper time. Wisdom always chooses God's will over everything else, and because of this, the life of the person who walks in wisdom is continually blessed.

LAZINESS

A lazy person looks for a way to avoid work. If he does work, he does as little as possible. Laziness is a shameful waste of the gifts and talents that God invests in us. We are created to be active, to handle responsibility, and to accomplish things. If we are not doing this because of laziness, we will be unhappy, though we may not know why.

We read that "ill-gotten treasures have no lasting value" (v. 2). If everything we need is handed to us or we compromise our morals to gain wealth that won't last, it will probably be wasted in a foolish and useless venture and then lost. Lazy hands lead to poverty, but diligent hands bring wealth (v. 4).

The wise person works hard to gather during times of harvest (plenty) and is considered to be prudent, but the one who is passive and lazy during those times is a disgrace (v. 5). For example, people whose work is seasonal must save money in their busy seasons so they will have the money they need during their slow seasons. In a town that thrives on tourism, businesses tend to be more profitable during travel seasons than during seasons when many people stay home. A wise person whose business caters to tourists would save during the busy times (harvest) so they will have plenty in the lean times. This requires not only wisdom but also prudence and discipline.

Honest, hard work is good for the soul. God created a beautiful garden for Adam to live in, but He gave him the job of tending, guarding, and keeping it (Genesis 2:15). God gives us many things, but if we do not do our part to maintain them, they will be lost or stolen by the enemy (Satan).

Other words for *laziness* are *slothful* and *passive*. A passive person would love for good things to happen to them and will sit idly by and wait to see if they do. I can tell you that with such an attitude, good never comes, because *nothing good happens accidentally*. Whatever God gives us to do, we are to do it with all of our heart as though we are doing it for Him alone (Colossians 3:23). I believe it dishonors God if we waste the gifts and abilities that He has made available to us through unwillingness to develop and work with them.

In the parable of the bags of gold, also known as the parable of the talents, found in Matthew 25:14–30, three servants are given sums of money (gold) and told to use them until the master comes back for an accounting. Two of them invest their money and have good returns to offer their master, but one of them hides his money because he is afraid. When the master returns, he rebukes the worker who hid his gold, saying he is a wicked, lazy, and idle servant and that what he has will be taken away from him and given to someone else. The basic principle of this story in contemporary language is, "Use it or lose it."

I urge you not to be lazy, but to be willing to work hard to develop and invest what God has given you. Many of us try to help our children by investing in their future as they get started in life, and it saddens us if they waste what we have given them. We want them to be grateful and to put our gifts to good use. God desires the same from us.

Even if you have less than others have when you get started, if you are grateful for what you have and you work hard, God will bless it and multiply it back to you many times over. This is a biblical principle: The diligent prosper, but laziness leads to poverty (v. 4).

INTEGRITY

"Whoever walks in integrity walks securely" (v. 9). People who have integrity in their hearts and in their actions make decisions that keep them safe, and the path they choose to walk through life leads them to many blessings. Integrity is related to honesty and means a firm adherence to a code or standard of values. It means "simplicity," "soundness," and "completeness" in the online Bible Dictionary (biblestudy tools.com). People with integrity are sincere and truthful, and they always keep their word.

You should say what you're going to do and do what you say. To be a person of integrity, you will need to keep your commitments even if it is inconvenient to do so. If for some valid reason you cannot do what you said you would do, then contact the person to whom you committed. Explain that your commitment was made in haste and that you should not have obligated yourself to it or let them know why you cannot keep your commitment at this time. Unforeseen situations do arise and prevent us from doing what we thought and said we would do. But because keeping our word is extremely important, we should never have a casual attitude about being unable to follow through on a commitment.

In one of Paul's apostolic prayers for the church, he prays that they will recognize "what is excellent and of real value" and remain "untainted and pure" by adhering to the excellent and best things (Philippians 1:10 AMPC). Being an excellent person is part of walking in integrity.

When Dave and I began our ministry more than forty years ago, God spoke to my heart about keeping the strife out of our lives, being excellent in all we do, and walking in integrity. He let me know that if we followed these wise principles, He would bless us and our ministry. We have made every effort to follow this time-honored wisdom, and our ministry and our lives have truly been blessed beyond my expectations.

God has called us to His own glory and excellence (2 Peter 1:3 AMPC). The word *glory* is a word we hear and use often as Christians, but do we know what it means? In the original languages of the Bible, it means the manifestation of all the excellencies of God. He is excellent, and as His followers, we should also be excellent in all we do. This means always going beyond what is expected and doing more than what is required. It means to do an excellent job at whatever we might be doing.

Most of us have dealt with the lack of excellence in the world today. It is difficult to find people who are committed to integrity and excellence. Our ministry conducted a survey, and we were shocked to find that many people today don't even know what *integrity* means. As believers, we need to understand integrity and to walk in it.

NO COMPROMISE

People with integrity do not compromise; they do the best job they can do even when no one is looking, because they realize that God is always watching and that their true reward comes from Him. To compromise is to do a little less than we should do or to go a little bit below what we know to be right, and it is easy to do. Although it's easy, we must avoid it.

Every time we compromise, it becomes easier to compromise again and again—and in more significant ways. If we are not careful, we will soon live a lifestyle filled with compromises. We may not even realize that a lifestyle of compromise is a problem, because we see so many other people doing the same thing. Always remember that we are not called to be like other people, but to be like Jesus.

Compromise causes us to be mediocre, and that causes problems for us. To be mediocre means to be halfway between good and bad, and it is the wrong place to be. Jesus says He would prefer that we either be hot or cold, not lukewarm (Revelation 3:15–16).

Many compromises seem to involve little things that don't matter much, but they do. We may compromise just a little, but little foxes spoil the vines (Song of Solomon 2:15 NKJV). One way Satan deceives us is to tell us that a little bit won't hurt us, but he is a liar. If we are faithful in little things, we can be trusted to be in charge of many things (Matthew 25:23).

Wisdom calls upon us to do what is right even if doing so seems to cost us, trusting that our reward will come at the proper time. God is the "rewarder of those who diligently seek Him" (Hebrews 11:6 NKJV).

Let me give you some practical examples of walking in integrity and doing things with excellence:

- Clean up any mess you make, and don't leave it for someone else to deal with.
- When performing a task, do the most excellent job you can do.

- Always keep your word. If you tell someone you will call them back, meet them at a certain time, or do something for them, then do it.
- Pay your bills on time. If for some reason you can't pay in a timely manner, be sure to communicate with the company you owe. Don't just ignore your responsibility.
- If you use the last tissue in the box, or the last of the toilet tissue on the roll, then replace it.
- If a store clerk gives you too much change when you purchase something, return the excess change to the store.
- If you purchase several items and later notice you were not charged for one of them, go back to the store and pay what you owe.
- Treat others as you would like to be treated (Matthew 7:12).
- Report to work on time.

There are thousands of other ways to live with integrity, some little and some big. Even seemingly small compromises can cause big problems and prevent us from being promoted in life.

Are you a person who understands and seeks to walk in integrity?

We are God's personal representatives, and He is making His appeal to the world through us (2 Corinthians 5:20); therefore, we must be committed to integrity and excellence.

THE POWER OF OUR WORDS

Proverbs 10 includes twelve references to the mouth, our words, or our lips. This subject is covered throughout the Book of Proverbs. I am going to cover the topic in greater detail in another chapter, but let me simply point out here that if one chapter contains twelve references to the subject, it surely must be important.

I think I can safely say that the words we speak have a far greater impact on our lives than most of us can imagine. James writes that no one can tame the tongue because "it is an unruly evil, full of deadly poison" (James 3:8 NKJV). We certainly cannot discipline our mouths without God's help, but nothing is impossible with Him (Luke 1:37), especially things He has commanded us to do or not to do. He will always help us follow His will if we truly desire to do so.

At times, we speak rashly and then wish we could take our words back. But once words are spoken, we cannot take them back. We may apologize for them, but even a profuse and sincere apology may not undo the damage thoughtless words have done.

Relationships are often ruined due to painful words that have been spoken or because of kind words left unspoken. Most people are starved for words of encouragement and edification, and if they never get them, it can cause loss of the relationship. Wise people store knowledge, but the mouth of a fool invites ruin (v. 14). The prudent (those who manage their lives wisely) hold their tongue (v. 19).

The words we speak come from the thoughts we think, and we are helpless to control our words if we let our thoughts run rampant. If we make sure to think godly thoughts, we will find godly words coming out of our mouth.

Words are containers for power, and we decide whether that power is creative or destructive. Wise people learn to think before they speak, but foolish ones destroy their lives with their words without knowing it. You will read more about this later, but for now I encourage you to begin pondering the truth that every word you speak holds some kind of power and to start praying and asking God to help you speak words filled with life and hope.

The Book of Proverbs is a wonderful book of the Bible, filled with practical wisdom for everyday living. Remember: Wise people do now what they will be satisfied with later in life. To walk in wisdom is to live without regret.

PROVERBS 11

The Lord detests dishonesty, and Proverbs 11 mentions that He hates dishonest weights and scales (v. 1). This is a reference to commerce or business practices in which a seller sets his scales to weigh incorrectly, thereby cheating the purchaser. I wrote extensively about integrity in chapter 10, and now, in Proverbs 11:3, Solomon mentions it, stating, "The integrity of the upright guides them, but the unfaithful are destroyed by their duplicity" (dishonesty). Anyone who cheats another person, thinking he is prospering by doing so, is deceived. Whatever we gain dishonestly, we always lose one way or another. It never blesses us.

THE DANGER OF PRIDE

Proverbs 11 mentions both pride and humility, which is the cure for pride: "When pride comes, then comes disgrace, but with humility comes wisdom" (v. 2). We learn in Proverbs 16:18 that pride goes before destruction, and Proverbs 13:10 teaches us that strife cannot exist without pride. If pride were eliminated from our lives, people would not fight and argue, and we would enjoy an abundance of peace. People tend to

crave being right, and out of their pride they stir up strife trying to prove they are right. One man I know admitted that he
had a problem with pride; every time he found himself in a
disagreement, he would argue and cause strife. He eventually
said, "Being right is highly overrated!" He realized the strife
it caused was not worth the momentary pleasure of thinking,
I'm right!

Dave and I once went shopping for a picture to hang on
a wall in our home. He found something he really liked, but
I didn't like it at all. I immediately became angry and started
arguing with him. He finally said in an aggravated tone, "Just
get what you want."

When we completed the purchase, I walked down the
mall feeling smug about getting my way. Then, the Lord
whispered to my heart, "You think you won, but you actually
lost." I quickly realized that the attitude I displayed in order
to get my way was ungodly and not pleasing to Him.

What should I have done in that situation? Since it
wasn't fair for either of us to live with a picture we didn't
like, Dave and I could have kept looking until we found one
that appealed to both of us. Most importantly, I should have
voiced my dislike in a respectful and loving manner rather
than the one I displayed.

Pride is an ugly attitude, and it is behind most of our ugly
reactions to people and situations. Our ego wants us to get
our way and wants to always be right, but relationships don't
work well under those circumstances. God tells us to humble
ourselves under His mighty hand and that in due time He
will exalt us (1 Peter 5:6).

Pride is birthed in our thoughts. We think more highly of ourselves than we ought to, but we should think of ourselves "with sober judgment," realizing that we are not always right and that other people's opinions are valuable (Romans 12:3). Only a fool refuses to listen to and consider ideas other than his own (Proverbs 12:15).

Proud, high-minded thinking can become strongholds in us—places where the enemy can gain access to our minds and establish his influence over our thoughts. The Word of God is an effective weapon for us to use in pulling down mental strongholds and breaking free from them (2 Corinthians 10:4). To be high-minded or haughty means to indulge in self-esteem or self-glorification or to glory in self-achievement. Please notice how often the word *self* appears as I describe haughtiness or high-mindedness. We should realize that any good we do is a manifestation of God's grace and goodness in our lives. He gives people gifts and abilities, and although we don't all have the same gifts, we all have gifts that are valuable and should be respected equally.

Are you willing to believe you could be wrong, even when you think you are right?

Boasting is a manifestation of pride, and it is the practice of quackery, pretending to be something that a person is not. It is created by high-mindedness. Proud and boastful people think they know what they do not know, and they think they are something that they are not.

GOD OPPOSES THE PROUD

God gives us grace to do what He wants us to do, but the grace only comes as we lean and rely on Him. Proud individuals who want to be self-reliant do not receive God's grace, but they do struggle in their own effort. James writes that God "gives us more grace" and that He "opposes the proud but shows favor to the humble" (James 4:6). In other words, God stands against the proud. Our flesh wants the credit for good things we do, but God will not share His glory with anyone (Isaiah 42:8).

Independent, self-sufficient boasters must be humbled before God can use them. This process is usually long and painful. Daniel 4:29–37 illustrates this through the story of King Nebuchadnezzar of Babylon. He began his reign giving God all the credit for his success, but before long he built a monument to himself and declared that he had done all the good things the people admired. The result was that he lost his kingdom and was "driven away from people and ate grass like the ox. His body was drenched with the dew of heaven until his hair grew like the feathers of an eagle and his nails like the claws of a bird" (Daniel 4:33). In other words, he lived in the open fields like a madman. However, he eventually came to his senses, and he blessed God and gave Him the glory due to Him. God gave him back his kingdom and his previous power and added even more greatness to him (Daniel 4:34–36). Nebuchadnezzar praised and honored the King of heaven, saying, "Everything he does is right and all his ways are just. And those who walk in pride he is able to humble" (Daniel 4:37).

PROMISES FOR THE RIGHTEOUS

Proverbs 11 includes twelve mentions of promises made to the righteous (vv. 4–31). The righteous are those who do what is right, meaning that they live according to God's Word. Therefore, we can say they are the ones who walk in wisdom. Doing what is right always brings a reward. We may have to exercise patience while we wait for our reward, but it will always come. Wisdom waits and thinks before it takes action. It follows peace and lives by the Word of God.

The righteous can trust in these promises:

1. They are delivered from death, probably referring to an untimely death (v. 4).
2. Their paths are made straight (v. 5).
3. They are delivered from the evil desires (v. 6).
4. They are rescued from trouble (v. 8).
5. They escape destruction (v. 9).
6. When they prosper and are blessed, the city they live in rejoices and is exalted (vv. 10–11).
7. They reap a sure reward (v. 18).
8. They attain life (v. 19).
9. They will experience freedom (v. 21).
10. Their desires end in good things (v. 23).
11. They will thrive (v. 28).

12. They will receive their due on earth (v. 31).

As you can see, the righteous can count on many wonderful promises. I don't want to miss out on them, and I'm sure you don't either.

In contrast to the promises made to the righteous, Proverbs 11 also includes promises to the wicked, also called "the unfaithful" and "the godless," but they are not things that anyone would want:

1.   They are "destroyed by their duplicity" (v. 3).
2.   They are "brought down by their own wickedness" (v. 5).
3.   They are "trapped by evil desires" (v. 6).
4.   Trouble falls on them (v. 8).
5.   They destroy their neighbors with their mouths (v. 9).
6.   When they perish, people shout for joy (v. 10).
7.   Their words destroy their cities (v. 11).
8.   They earn their wages through deceit (v. 18).
9.   They find death (v. 19; again, probably referring to an early death).
10. They do not go unpunished (v. 21).
11. Their hope ends only in wrath (v. 23).
12. Like the righteous, they also find their due on earth, but it will not be anything they can enjoy (v. 31).

It seems to me that the choice concerning which way to live is obvious, yet countless people seem uninterested in righteousness and choose the wicked way—the ungodly way—instead. They do what they feel like doing without thinking about the future consequences of their actions. Our time on earth—even if we live to be one hundred years old—is like a grain of sand compared to eternity. We should live for eternity rather than for the present moment. I'll say it again: We need to do now what we will be satisfied with later.

Hebrews 12:11 says that to do what is right when we don't feel like doing it requires self-discipline. It may not feel joyous while we are exercising it, but later on it yields a "harvest of righteousness and peace."

GENEROSITY AND KINDNESS

Proverbs 11 states that kindness and generosity benefit us (vv. 17, 24–25). A generous person prospers. Those who are generous give out of what they have and end up with more than they started with before they gave. This type of math only works in God's kingdom. In the world's system, people who want more must save or take from others. But in God's kingdom, if we want more then we have to give some of what we have. We have to temporarily lose in order to gain. In the end, givers never lose! It is impossible to outgive God's generosity to us.

Are you generous to others?

Our giving to others refreshes them and increases their faith, and when we refresh others, we are refreshed ourselves

(v. 25). I have discovered that when I am unhappy, I can quickly find joy by simply planning to do something to bless someone else. Most unhappiness is derived from selfishness; therefore, being unselfish fixes the problem.

Don't live to get, but live to give—and it will provide you with a blessed life that you can truly enjoy.

PROVERBS 12

I n agreement with the theme of the entire Book of Proverbs, Proverbs 12 confirms repeatedly that the righteous or wise person will be blessed in many ways, but the wicked or foolish one will come to poverty and experience lifelong troubles. Thank God that we have a choice about how we behave and the lives we want to live. Joshua 24:15 says, "If serving the Lord seems undesirable to you, then *choose for yourselves this day whom you will serve,* whether the gods your ancestors served beyond the Euphrates, or the gods of the Amorites, in whose land you are living. But as for me and my household, we will serve the Lord" (emphasis mine).

I love the firm way in which Joshua declares his choice to serve God no matter what anyone else does. He also makes clear that everyone has a choice concerning whether to serve the Lord or not, just as he does. Each of us has the privilege of making our own decisions, and we should firmly resist allowing anyone to entice us in the wrong direction.

Another scripture that emphasizes the fact that we can exercise free choice is Deuteronomy 30:19: "This day I call the heavens and the earth as witnesses against you that I have set before you life and death, blessings and curses. Now choose life, so that you and your children may live." God not only gives us a choice, but He also tells us which choice to make if we want to enjoy a good life. We can follow God, or we can follow fleshly desires, but we should remember that we will reap what we sow (Galatians 6:7). In other words, all of our choices will have consequences and we can know from God's Word what they will be.

Proverbs 12 begins with a direct statement: "Whoever loves discipline loves knowledge, but whoever hates correction is stupid" (v. 1). It is difficult to find people who truly love and appreciate correction. Our fleshly tendency toward rebellion resists correction, but a wise person learns to appreciate it. We cannot gain knowledge without learning to discipline the flesh. No matter how much you think you know, just imagine how much you don't know that you could know if you would receive discipline and correction as blessings from God.

There are, of course, people who try to correct us for wrong reasons or in inappropriate ways. I am not saying we need to receive correction from just anyone who wants to dish it out. But when correction comes from God's Word or from godly people we trust, we should be glad to receive it. Pride causes us to think we know more than we do, but humility will always listen and consider the validity of godly correction offered in the right spirit.

GOD'S FAVOR

God's favor is wonderful to experience, and Proverbs 12:2 teaches us that a good person obtains the favor of God. In

Psalm 5:12 we read, "Surely, Lord, you bless the righteous; you surround them with your favor as with a shield." These scriptures and similar ones offer us the joyful message that we can live in God's favor.

When we live under the blessing of God's favor, we find people doing special things for us for no reason at all—except that God has given us favor. His favor opens doors for us, giving us opportunities we would not otherwise have. God's favor also promotes us. Just imagine being surrounded by God's favor and how it would make your life much more enjoyable and exciting.

Who doesn't want or need a favor at times? Have you ever said to anyone, "Can you do me a favor?" I am sure that you have, and I have, too. It might be something like, "Can you do me a favor and help me move on Saturday?" or, "Can you do me a favor and give me a ride to work tomorrow because my car is in the shop?" We all need favors now and then, and when someone does us a favor, we appreciate it. As nice as it may be to have favor with a person, having favor with God is so much better. It is truly amazing.

God's favor gives you what you don't really deserve because you have not earned it. Grace is God's favor! By grace we are saved through faith (Ephesians 2:8–9). Salvation itself is a favor from God. Everything we receive from God is received through faith, so I recommend that you release your faith to begin living in the favor of God. Look up all the scriptures on God's favor and start confessing (speaking aloud) that you have God's favor everywhere you go. Then begin watching His favor work on your behalf. Confessing God's Word is one way to release your faith, and praying is another, so pray and ask God to give you His favor. We forfeit many of God's blessings simply because we fail to ask for them (James 4:2).

Another way to attract God's favor is to do favors for others. A righteous person shows kindness, even to animals (v. 10). God is kind and good to all, and we should emulate His behavior. Simply being kind doesn't cost anything, but it pays great benefits and rewards. Those who are kind benefit themselves (Proverbs 11:17). If we sow kindness, we will reap kindness. We should always be willing to go out of our way to do favors for people, remembering that those favors will come back to us. Anytime we give, we bless ourselves in addition to blessing the recipient of our gift. We never lose through giving; we always gain.

DON'T CHASE FANTASIES

Proverbs 12:11 says, "Those who work their land will have abundant food, but those who chase fantasies have no sense." People who chase fantasies think they can do wrong and still be blessed. We often hear them say, "I wish thus-and-so would happen to me," but good things rarely come to us by wishing. Good things come by applying the principles of God's Word, including those we find in the Book of Proverbs, such as wisdom, understanding, knowledge, discernment, discretion, prudence, and the fear of the Lord. We are chasing fantasies if we think we can be lazy and prosper, or if we believe we can mistreat people and have a lot of friends, or if we allow ourselves to think we can abuse our bodies and be healthy. However, if we apply God's principles consistently in our lives, we will reap the rewards that He promises us. We are to be sober minded and serious, realizing what is at stake if we don't follow God and obey Him.

THE POWER OF POSITIVE SPEAKING

Proverbs 12 includes several verses regarding how we speak. One promise we find for those who speak wisely is that their tongue will bring healing (v. 18). If we ponder this, we realize we can apply it in many different ways. Our words can bring healing to broken relationships, they can comfort and bring healing to those who have wounded souls, and I believe that words can even bring physical healing to those whose bodies are sick. Proverbs 16:24 says, "Gracious words are a honeycomb, sweet to the soul and healing to the bones." Many sick people make the mistake of speaking negatively and voicing fear regarding their illness, but we can declare that Christ is our Healer and that He is working in us every day (Philippians 2:13; 1 Peter 2:24). "A cheerful heart is good medicine," Proverbs 17:22 says, so speaking happy and positive words can be very healing and helpful to those who are ill. Studies have shown that the more positive a sick person is, the more likely they are to get well. Foolish people talk too much and revel in telling others what they know, but

> *Would you say that you speak positively in all circumstances?*

prudent people "keep their knowledge to themselves" (v. 23). A friend of mine was married to a very intelligent man who tended to be rather quiet. One time after a gathering where people were discussing and debating a specific subject that he happened to know a lot about, his wife asked him why he didn't tell everyone what he knew. His answer was brilliant. He said, "Because I already know what I know. I was listening to see if I could learn anything else." Now, that is a wise man!

ANXIETY

Anxiety is a significant problem for millions of people. In fact, according to the Anxiety and Depression Society of America, almost 40 million people over the age of eighteen in the United States struggle with anxiety disorders. As wickedness (ungodliness) increases in the world, anxiety multiplies. Society, jobs, family, and friends can place seemingly overwhelming expectations on us at times, and we easily find many things to worry about unless we know it is useless to do so. We don't have to worry; we can trust God instead. However, it takes a child of God time to learn how to do that. Unfortunately, some never learn it and struggle with anxiety for many years.

Proverbs 12:25 teaches us that anxiety in a person's heart weighs it down, "but a kind word cheers it up." This verse shows us how to help people, and the way to do so is through kindness, especially by speaking kind words. Speaking words of kindness is a way of blessing and giving to others.

Instead of putting undue stress on people by using your words to pressure them to be perfect or to please you all the time, speak in ways that show them mercy and cover their offenses. The Bible says that "love covers over a multitude of sins" (1 Peter 4:8). Wise people are not harsh when speaking to those who have made mistakes or disappointed them, because they know they have done the same to others, probably many times.

We are to treat people as we want to be treated (Luke 6:31). Just imagine how much better life would be if everyone did that. One of the best gifts we can give people is simple: sincere kindness. When you know someone who is anxious and worried, comfort and encourage them with positive words and acts of kindness that will help the situation as much as possible. If a person is worried because they couldn't pay their rent last month, maybe you could pay it for them. These kinds of opportunities and thousands of others frequently present themselves to us. Foolish people allow these opportunities to pass by, but the wise make the most of them.

CHOOSE YOUR FRIENDS WISELY

"The righteous choose their friends carefully, but the way of the wicked leads them astray" (v. 26). Many people could quickly change their lives for the better by simply getting some new friends. The people with whom we spend our time are very important because they influence us. The more we are around them, the more we may begin to think and act as they do. If they are godly and wise, their influence on us is beneficial. But if they are not, then we have to make sure that we are *affecting* them in positive ways and that they are not *infecting* us with their negative ways. Let me encourage you to take time to really think about the people you spend most of your time with. Are they people you want to be like? If not, then choose friends who are.

The Old Testament character Daniel was godly, wise, and filled with integrity; so were his closest friends. We can tell a lot about people by the individuals with whom they surround themselves. We do want to minister to those who do not know the Lord and influence their lives in positive ways, but as I noted earlier, we have to make sure we are affecting them instead of allowing them to infect us.

Proverbs 13:20 gives us even more insight into this matter: "Walk with the wise and become wise, for a companion of fools suffers harm." If you have no choice but to be with people who are foolish and ungodly, at work or in your family, pray that you will not be influenced by them and make sure you have plenty of wise, godly friends to help offset the others.

Second Corinthians 6:17 calls us to "come out from them and be separate." We live our lives in the world, but we are not to be like the world (John 17:16). This does not mean that we mistreat ungodly people or behave as though we think we

> *Do you need some new friends?*

are better than they are. It does, however, admonish us to be careful not to let them affect us negatively. Jesus regularly ate with sinners and people who the religious elite of His day totally rejected. He did so because He loved them and wanted them to know the truth. He never allowed them to influence Him, and He always spoke boldly about truth and God's will.

Let me encourage you to spend as much time as possible with people you admire and want to be like. As you have opportunities to be around them, you will begin to emulate their habits and behaviors.

PROVERBS 13

As I studied to write this book, I became more impressed than ever concerning the importance of wisdom. As I have noted previously, I believe wisdom is doing now what we will be satisfied with later. But we live such fast-paced lives that I believe we miss many lessons and advice that would benefit us if we would slow down. In Proverbs 13, Solomon repeats matters he has written about previously. Proverbs is full of topics mentioned several times, so God apparently thinks repetition is important in order for us to learn what He is trying to teach us. I have certainly learned that each time we hear the Word or meditate on it, it becomes more deeply rooted in us, and the enemy has more difficulty taking it from us through his lies and deceptions.

One of the first subjects Solomon addresses in Proverbs 13 is the fruit of our lips, meaning our words. Verse 2 says, "From the fruit of their lips people enjoy good things, but the unfaithful have an appetite for violence." Verse 3 continues: "Those who guard their lips preserve their lives, but those who speak rashly will come to ruin." I'm sure we can all say amen to that! Learning to slow down and think before we speak benefits us in many ways.

Solomon now reminds us that a lazy person's appetite "is never filled, but the desires of the diligent are fully satisfied" (v. 4). Every generation encounters new problems, and one problem we are facing today is that some young people have an attitude of entitlement. They think they deserve what they have not worked for and should have things they make no effort to obtain. I come from a generation of people who expected to work hard

> *Do you often say things and then wish you hadn't said them?*

if we wanted to have anything, and I personally think that mentality was good for me. How can we truly appreciate anything if we put no work into getting it? When we work and wait for something, only then can we truly appreciate its value. Lazy people want everything, but they want someone else to expend the effort needed to get it. That is not God's plan and will not work.

In addition to entitled young people, there are also many wonderful, godly young men and women who are passionate for Christ and godly living. Hopefully they will have a positive effect on their peers and become good examples to them. I am greatly encouraged when I hear or read about young people who are learning to work hard, save their money, and live within their means, because they are setting themselves up for a lifetime of success as they continue walking in wisdom.

THE RIGHTEOUS

Throughout the Book of Proverbs we see that many promises are made to the righteous. So far, I have not found one single benefit to being wicked (doing wrong), but there are many benefits to being righteous (doing right). Proverbs 13 tells us that "righteousness guards the person of integrity" (v. 6). It protects them from harm and evil. "The light of the righteous shines brightly, but the lamp of the wicked is snuffed out"(v. 9). Jesus says that we are the light of the world and that we should let our lights shine (Matthew 5:14–16). This simply means we are to display the character of Christ in the world around us. When our light shines, people who need Jesus are drawn to us and we have opportunities to minister to them. The world is full of darkness (sin and evil), and darkness can only be overcome by light (John 1:5). So wherever you go, whatever you do, be sure to let your light shine and to represent Jesus well.

"The righteous are rewarded with good things" (v. 21). Doing the right thing now brings a reward later. Proverbs 13:25 says that when the righteous eat food, they "eat to their hearts' content, but the stomach of the wicked goes hungry."

Under the Old Covenant (meaning during Old Testament times), people had to make every effort to do what was right in order to be considered righteous. They could never keep all the laws perfectly; therefore, a system was instituted in which the high priest could offer sacrifices for the people's sins. Although the sins were never removed, they could be covered. Proverbs was written while the Old Testament law was still in effect, so when it mentions "the righteous" it refers to those who tried hard to do what was right and followed the laws as best as they could, regularly making sacrifices to cover their sin.

Under the New Covenant, Jesus, our high priest, became our sacrifice for sin. He personally took the punishment we deserved because of our sin, died on the cross, went to hell, and was raised from the dead on the third day, securing our freedom from sin. By His sacrifice we "become the righteousness of God" in Christ (2 Corinthians 5:21). We can do what is right because we have been made right. We still make mistakes, but we never lose our right standing with God as long as we repent of our sins and want to do what is right according to His Word.

PRETENSE

God wants us to be genuine and honest in all our ways. But Proverbs 13:7 tells us that there are people who pretend to be rich yet have nothing, and there are those who pretend to be poor, yet they are rich. We may wonder why people would act in these ways, but they do. I have had people tell me they can't afford to do something Dave and I have invited them to do, and we have paid for them to join us. Later I discovered that they had plenty of money; they simply didn't want to spend it. This kind of pretense is actually lying, and that is not something we should do. The people should have said, "We don't want to spend the money to do that," instead of pretending they didn't have it. As Proverbs 13:7 teaches us, there are also people who pretend to be rich even though they are poor because they are ashamed that they do not have as much as other people. Regardless of the reason for it, pretense is never honorable. God delights in and honors those who are honest and sincere.

The root cause of pretense is often insecurity, but we can be confident and secure in God's love for us. We have no need to pretend to be anything other than what and who we truly are. When I finally got away from my abusive father, I pretended to be bold and aggressive. I gave the impression that I didn't need anyone, but the truth was that I was broken, frightened, and insecure. I wanted desperately to be loved and to have people to lean on.

I've learned over the years that God loves me the way I am and that I don't need to pretend to be anyone other than who I am. I encourage you also not to behave one way with some people and another way with others you may want to impress. Be genuine and avoid showing favoritism to people (Romans 2:11; James 2:1). Instead, be like Jesus, who accepts others just as they are.

HOPE

Hope is much more than most people think. It isn't a *wish* that things would get better, but *a belief and an expectation* that they *will* get better. "Hope deferred makes the heart sick" (v. 12), which means that hopelessness makes you discouraged and depressed. But hope empowers you to press on joyfully, knowing that your circumstance will eventually give way to the power of faith and trust in God. Hope is an aggressive expectation that something good is going to happen to you at any minute. A hopeful person wakes up each day and says, "Something good is going to happen to me today."

The Old Testament prophet Zechariah writes about "prisoners of hope" (Zechariah 9:12). This term refers to people who are so hopeful that nothing can take their hope away from them. God promises that He will restore "twice as much" to them. Anyone can have a negative, sour attitude and assume things will go from bad to worse, but those filled with the Spirit of God can, by faith, believe in God's promises and be hopeful that the future looks good.

Hope is the anchor of our souls (Hebrews 6:19). When our thoughts and emotions could be tossed up and down with our changing circumstances, hope anchors us to the promises of God. It keeps us stable and steady until our breakthroughs come. We might say that hope is a positive attitude, and we need to realize that our attitudes belong to us. No one can make us have a bad attitude if we don't want one.

Decide today to be full of hope in every situation you encounter and you will see a positive change in your level of joy.

GOOD JUDGMENT

A person who uses good judgment "wins favor, but the way of the unfaithful leads to their destruction" (v. 15). People with good judgment consider all their options before making decisions. They weigh their choices, look at the pros and cons, and then make their decisions after waiting on wisdom and giving their emotions time to settle.

Prudence is a display of good management, and it has a lot to do with good judgment. When we are judging whether or not to do something or buy something, we have to examine whether or not we can manage it. For example, it does no good to get a pay raise if you don't intend to manage the additional money well. It is useless to take a promotion involving greater responsibility at work if you cannot manage your current responsibilities well.

Years ago, while Dave was a draftsman for an engineering company, he was offered a promotion, but he turned it down. I was a bit upset at first and asked, "Why don't you want to advance?" He told me that the increase in pay was very small and the promotion would mean he would have a lot more responsibility and need to travel part of the time. When he declined the promotion, he acted wisely.

Everything that looks or feels good at first is not always an opportunity that will ultimately benefit us. Sometimes all we do is take on more stress simply because we don't have the courage to say no to an opportunity. "All who are prudent act with knowledge, but fools expose their folly" (v. 16).

CORRECTION AND DISCIPLINE

"Whoever disregards discipline comes to poverty and shame, but whoever heeds correction is honored" (v. 18). Many people love to dole out discipline or give correction, but they are not good at taking it. Pride causes us to avoid correction, often by blaming a problem on someone else. "I wouldn't if you didn't," becomes an easy excuse for not examining our personal behavior. Each of us is responsible before God for our own actions, no matter what anyone else does. Therefore we should not make excuses but humbly receive correction and let it do its work in us. I know this is easier said than done, but prayer allows us to access God's power, which enables us to do with ease what would otherwise be impossible. If we cannot humble ourselves before people, we will not be able to humble ourselves before God. If we cannot receive correction from people, neither will we receive it from God. In many cases, God works through people to bring us the correction we need. When we need to be corrected, He begins privately, but if we won't listen and respond, He will correct us publicly.

> *Do you receive correction well, or do you resist it?*

WHAT KIND OF LEGACY ARE YOU LEAVING?

"A good person leaves an inheritance for their children's children, but a sinner's wealth is stored up for the righteous"

(v. 22). When we think of leaving an inheritance, we usually think of bequeathing money to our children. Financial resources certainly can be an inheritance, but we can also leave other things as part of our legacy, things that are actually more important than money.

I'm sad to say that because of the alcoholism and abuse in my family, I never remember my parents intentionally trying to teach me any kind of good and moral principle that would have helped me prepare for adulthood. Thankfully, I learned these lessons from my heavenly Father and from His Word.

Dave and I are saving financially to leave our children and grandchildren an inheritance, but in addition to that, I occasionally write my four children what I call a legacy letter. In these letters, I share with them important life principles that I believe will really help them. When I am gone from this world, they can reread these letters, share them with their children, and keep learning from me. Our children often talk about things they have learned from Dave and me, and it always pleases me to know we taught them good, godly values.

Parents make a strong impact on their children. What we say to them is important, but what they see us do is even more important. Don't tell your children not to lie and then tell them to say you are not home when the phone rings and you don't want to take the call. Don't tell them never to steal and then brag about finding a way to cheat on your income tax. Whatever you want your children to display in terms of character and behavior, you need to model as you live your life in front of them.

SPARE THE ROD
AND SPOIL THE CHILD

Many people have heard Proverbs 13:24 paraphrased to say, "Spare the rod and spoil the child" and wondered what it means. The NIV makes its meaning clear: "Whoever spares the rod hates their children, but the one who loves their children is careful to discipline them" (v. 24). Some of us have heard this proverb quoted, especially when we were children and a parent was about to give us a spanking—or in some cases a beating. Many parents have taken this scripture out of context and used it as an excuse to use violence against their children, and that is definitely not what God had in mind.

What is the "rod" about which Solomon writes? It was a long stick shepherds used to tap the legs of the sheep when they veered off the path. They did not beat the sheep with it, as some parents have done to their children. My father slapped me in the face when he was angry, but that did not correct me; it only made me afraid of him. He also beat me with his belt if I did something that made him *really* angry. That kind of treatment is not God's will, nor does it help a child. Many parents today find that taking away a privilege when a child needs to be corrected is more effective than hitting them would be. We cannot teach our children not to hit others and then hit them ourselves.

Dave and I did spank our children, because spanking was the form of discipline we were taught to use. But if I were raising children today, I think I might do things differently.

Spanking as a form of punishment is a very controversial subject, and parents must decide for themselves with God's direction how they want to discipline their children.

I called my daughter who has four children to ask for her thoughts on this matter. She mentioned that one of her children (my grandchild) is very tender in nature, and that a spanking would have devastated her. She also said that one of her other children was quite stubborn and nothing seemed to stop her from misbehaving. During one period of her toddler years, that child started biting people, and nothing her parents tried made her quit. Finally my daughter bit her back, and she never bit anyone again after that.

A parent might slap a child's hand to keep them from getting it too close to a fire or a hot stove burner, but that is not done as a form of discipline. Such action is taken in love to keep the child from further harm and is entirely different from beating them.

An important lesson to learn about disciplining children is to do it when you can be reasonable and think wisely and maturely about it. When you need to correct your child, I strongly urge you not to do it in anger. Wait until you calm down, and don't let your emotions guide your correction.

Sometimes God's correction hurts, but He is never abusive. God has never made me sick or brought disaster into my life to teach me anything. He teaches us in many ways, but abuse is not one of them.

PROVERBS 14

Proverbs 14 continues to remind us that wise people—those who follow God's ways—will always flourish and be blessed. But fools—those who don't follow God's ways—find nothing but destruction. I have written already about the fact that wisdom must be waited on, and Proverbs 14:8 says, "The wisdom of the prudent is to give thought to their ways." Proverbs 14:6 says that "knowledge comes easily to the discerning," but once again, discernment comes as we wait on God and ponder the right course of action to take. Neither wisdom nor discernment comes from random thoughts; they are treasures hidden in our spirit just waiting to be brought to light for those who are willing to seek them.

I would like to highlight three main points in Proverbs 14: the fear of the Lord, the dangers of anger, and the importance of living in peace.

THE REVERENTIAL FEAR AND AWE OF GOD

Proverbs 14:2 says, "Whoever fears the Lord walks uprightly, but those who despise him are devious in all their ways."

Those who have reverential fear and a respectful awe of God are obedient to Him. Once again, this does not mean that if we fear God, we should be afraid that He will hurt us or reject us if we don't do everything just right. It does mean that we respect God enough to do all we can to please Him.

A practical example of this would be when several employees in a business are talking in a group and the boss walks up to them. They usually disperse quickly and get back to work. Or, if someone is on a personal phone call and sees the boss nearby, they will quickly hang up and get back to work. This is because most people have a reverential fear of their employer. They know he has the power to promote them or to demote them. That same kind of power belongs to God to an infinitely greater degree. It is important for us to do what we know He would want us to do at all times. Our employers may not be watching us constantly, but God is, and keeping that in mind helps us maintain holy lives.

God doesn't want to have to give us continual instructions on what to do. He has given us every instruction we will ever need in His Word. He prefers that we know Him well enough to know what He approves or disapproves of and then do it without being told. Our goal should be to live with and for God and His will, not to live our own lives and then expect Him to get us out of trouble when following our own ways gets us into trouble.

"There is a way that appears to be right, but in the end it leads to death" (v. 12). This is an important scripture for us to keep in mind. We need to realize that just because something feels right to us, it doesn't mean that it is right. This is why we need to slow down and wait on wisdom and discernment. We need to wait for God to bear witness with our conscience that our intended actions are right or wrong. There are times when I want to do something and I don't sense that anything would be wrong with doing it, yet I still cannot find peace about it. To me, this means that God wants me to do something differently, and I need to patiently wait for His direction. Those who fear the Lord are willing to wait on Him.

Proverbs 14:26 says, "Whoever fears the Lord has a secure fortress, and for their children it will be a refuge." Not only do we benefit from the wisdom of fearing the Lord appropriately, but our children benefit as well. Not only do we have to wait on wisdom; we also often have to wait on the reward that is ours because of it. All waiting can be considered a time of testing. It is easy to keep obeying God when blessings are flowing in our lives, but when our obedience to God appears to be doing no good, continuing to obey can become difficult.

Let me encourage you to do what is right not just because you think you will get a reward of some kind. Do what is right because it is right and because you know it pleases God.

Proverbs 14:27 says, "The fear of the Lord is a fountain of life, turning a person from the snares of death." It saddens me to think about how many people have no understanding of the fear of the Lord. Because of this, they compromise their morals and assume that God will overlook their lack of obedience because He is good and gracious.

God is good, but He is also just. His Word says that He is both kind and stern (Romans 11:22). The Lord is always ready to forgive those who repent, and they will experience

His kindness, but those who continue in sin without repentance will experience the severity of God. However, even when He deals with someone in a stern manner, He still does it out of His great love, hoping to motivate that person to right living.

BE SLOW TO ANGER

The Word of God is filled with instructions about the dangers of anger. In the Old Testament, Moses made some ill-fated decisions due to his anger and was not allowed to enter the Promised Land because of them (Deuteronomy 32:51–52). In the New Testament, the apostle James writes: "My dear brothers and sisters, take note of this: Everyone should be quick to listen, slow to speak and slow to become angry, because human anger does not produce the righteousness that God desires" (James 1:19–20).

Solomon writes in Proverbs 14:17, "A quick-tempered person does foolish things." Later in this chapter, he writes that a "quick-tempered" person "displays folly" (v. 29). He also writes in Ecclesiastes 7:9, "Do not be quickly provoked in your spirit, for anger resides in the lap of fools." I am sure we can all think of times when, because of anger, we have done and said foolish things and wish we had not.

I have said many times, "Let emotions subside before you decide," meaning that people should not make decisions based on strong feelings. Anger is definitely an emotion we should allow to subside before we decide on a course of action. Remembering this is helpful in disciplining our children. Doling out punishment when we are angry almost always results in punishment too extreme for the offense the child committed. I can remember correcting my children in anger and saying things like, "You are grounded for thirty days!" After about three days, I realized I was punishing myself more than the children, because I ended up stuck in the house as they made noise all day. So I would then release them from the grounding early, which made me look unstable and easy to manipulate.

Dave handled situations requiring discipline differently. When he needed to correct our children, he told them he would think about what their punishment should be and tell them when he decided. He considered the appropriate discipline, told them what it was, and never backed down. They, of course, had reverential fear of Dave because they knew he meant what he said, but they knew I could be talked into changing my mind.

The subject of anger is one we should take very seriously. God never tells us not to ever get angry, but He does say that when we are angry, we should avoid sin. His Word also says not to let the sun set on our anger so we will not give the devil a foothold in (access to) our lives (Ephesians 4:26–27). We see from these verses that uncontrolled anger can cause us to sin. People have even committed murder in moments of anger and spent the rest of their lives in prison because of one angry moment and no self-control.

I think we can agree that, generally speaking, we live in an angry society. I can certainly say that today more people are angry than I have ever seen in my lifetime. Sometimes I feel that some people are sitting on a powder keg of dynamite just waiting for an opportunity to explode. When Jesus speaks about the end times, one of the signs He mentions is that many would be "offended" and "pursue one another with hatred" or "hate one another" (Matthew 24:10 AMPC, NKJV, KJV). Other translations say that people will "turn away" or "fall away" from their faith in Christ and hate one another (NIV, NLT, ESV, NASB). Anger is a real emotion and we all experience it, but thankfully Jesus gives us a solution to it, which is to forgive just as He has forgiven us (Mark 11:25; Luke 11:4).

> When you are angry, do you forgive quickly or harbor resentment?

Some people think that forgiving others is so difficult that they choose instead to remain angry. But living with anger in our hearts is much more difficult than forgiving. When we forgive others, we set ourselves free from the agony and burden of carrying hatred, bitterness, and resentment. Being a person who is quick to forgive is a great blessing and pleases God.

LIVE IN PEACE

"A heart at peace gives life to the body, but envy rots the bones" (v. 30). This is a wonderful scripture that teaches us great practical lessons. Living in peace keeps us healthy, but emotions that destroy our peace can cause sickness. Negative emotions place stress on us, and too much stress over a long period of time causes many illnesses.

I grew up in a house filled with turmoil and can honestly say that I didn't even know what peace felt like. After Dave and I married and I observed his life over a period of time, I began to realize that the peace he had was worth whatever I had to do to get it. And I needed to make a lot of changes over a period of several years before I could say I lived in peace most of the time.

Peace is something we must pursue, seek, and search for (1 Peter 3:11 NIV, AMP). The enemy sets us up to get us upset because he knows that when we are upset, we make mistakes. We say things we should not say and do things we should not do. He also knows that a lack of peace erodes our health. Jesus says that He has left us His peace, not peace "as the world gives," but His own special peace; because of that, we should stop allowing ourselves to be "agitated and disturbed" (John 14:27 AMPC). John 14:27 indicates that we can control ourselves if we really want to. Anyone can find many, many things to worry about, but we don't have to. We have the option of turning our problems over to God and trusting Him to take care of us.

One way to maintain peace is to really think about whether or not being upset will do you any good. Will it solve your problem? Will it change anything? No, it won't. Ephesians 6 teaches us to put on the armor that God has given us in order to defeat the wicked powers at work in the world. Part of that armor includes the shoes of peace. The Scripture tells us to have our feet "fitted with the readiness that comes from the gospel of peace" (Ephesians 6:15). Staying peaceful is one of the best ways to defeat the enemy. Remember, he wants you to be upset, so disappoint him and hold on to your peace. Jesus is the Prince of Peace, and He will help you enjoy peace at all times if you will listen to Him and let Him guide you in all situations. As soon as you feel angry, start praying and asking God to help you calm down.

In Exodus 14, we read that the Israelites were trapped between the Egyptian army and the Red Sea. In that terrible situation, they cried out to Moses for help. He told them to stand still, not be afraid, and hold their peace, and God would fight for them and destroy their enemies (Exodus 14:13–14). When we hold our peace in situations that could upset us, we are showing God that we trust Him, and He goes to work on our behalf and brings us into victory.

I hope you have learned valuable lessons about the fear of the Lord, the dangers of anger, and the importance of living at peace from Proverbs 14. Take these lessons to heart and incorporate them into your life so you can experience their benefits right away.

PROVERBS 15

Proverbs 15 begins with one of my favorite Bible verses: "A gentle answer turns away wrath, but a harsh word stirs up anger" (v. 1). One reason I like this scripture so much is that gentleness was not a natural trait for me, but one I had to develop with God's help. If people spoke to me harshly, my natural tendency was to lash out in response to them, but that is not God's way. Later in Proverbs 15, verse 18 makes a similar point: "A hot-tempered person stirs up conflict, but the one who is patient calms a quarrel."

Staying calm and answering someone gently when that person speaks angrily to us may be difficult to do, but answering someone who is upset in a calm and gentle way helps to calm down a situation. However, if we return anger for anger, we only increase the level of tension for everyone involved. God is wise, and all of His instructions for us in handling situations are intended to make our lives more peaceful and enjoyable.

Jesus dealt with many harsh people—those who accused Him of evil things, those who wanted to kill Him, and those whose goal was to stir up trouble for Him—yet He always answered them calmly with gentleness, or didn't answer them at all but simply walked away (Matthew 27:14; Mark 14:61; John 19:9).

Paul teaches us: "If it is possible, as far as it depends on you, live at peace with everyone" (Romans 12:18). In tense situations, we are not to passively wait for others to try to make peace with us, but we are to do everything possible to make and maintain peace with everyone. I believe that when two people are angry and upset with each other, the one who is willing to apologize and try to make peace first is the one who is most spiritually mature.

God's grace and blessing abide where peace and unity are (Psalm 133). Jesus says that people who make peace "will be called children of God" (Matthew 5:9). Jesus "himself is our peace" (Ephesians 2:14). We are imitating Christ when we love peace and do all we can to promote it. Perhaps nothing is more challenging than attempting to remain calm when we are falsely accused. No one enjoys being yelled at or spoken to in harsh and disrespectful tones of voice, yet Jesus was able to withstand it and remain at peace. Behaving as He did in the face of such attacks takes a great deal of humility.

I had a friend whose son was quite belligerent with her. Over time, she found that the best way to deal with him was not to answer him at all in certain situations. She said the silence she allowed gave God an opportunity to confront her son with his own words. After having a moment to think about what he had said and how angrily he had spoken to her, he often apologized. However, if she became angry and began to argue with him, it escalated the situation into a full-blown shouting match that never changed anything. I think the reason Jesus often did not answer His accusers was that He knew that responding would be useless and the silence left them to deal with the foolishness of their false accusations. Whether you use gentle words to dispel anger or say nothing at all, one thing is for sure: Heated arguing never does any good.

WORDS THAT UPLIFT
AND BRING COMFORT

Proverbs 15 contains seven references to the words we speak. I want to highlight and draw lessons from two of them. The first one is, "The soothing tongue is a tree of life, but a perverse tongue crushes the spirit" (v. 4). Just as gentle words calm an angry person, soothing words can comfort one who is hurting or upset. They bring life, and that always means something good. I can't think of anyone who doesn't appreciate a kind and uplifting word, and people need these words more than we may realize. We need them also, perhaps more than we realize.

God's Word tells us often to be encouraging and to edify one another. Here are a few examples:

Therefore encourage one another and build each other up, just as in fact you are doing.

1 Thessalonians 5:11

Do not let any unwholesome talk come out of your mouths, but only what is helpful for building others up according to their needs, that it may benefit those who listen.

Ephesians 4:29

Not giving up meeting together, as some are in the habit of doing, but encouraging one another—and all the more as you see the Day approaching.

Hebrews 10:25

Other words the Bible uses to express encouragement are *edify* and *exhort*. These words mean to strengthen, to help another continue making progress, to give support, and to stimulate. Hebrews 10:25 teaches us as believers to encourage each other even more as the Day approaches. "The Day" the writer refers to is the second coming of Christ. God's Word tells us that great difficulty will arise on earth prior to the second coming of Christ (Matthew 24:3–31). The more difficult our lives are, the more encouragement we need.

Do you make it your aim to encourage people everywhere you go? I hope you

> *Do you make an effort to speak encouraging words to the people around you?*

do, but if not, you can begin today. Many people say they want to be used by God, and this is one way that desire can be fulfilled. Never underestimate the value of a soothing and encouraging comment. It is one of the best ways you can use your words.

The second scripture on which I want to focus is Proverbs 15:23: "A person finds joy in giving an apt reply—and how good is a timely word!" According to this verse, those who encourage others find joy in doing so. This confirms the fact that our words not only affect others, but they also affect us. To put it plainly, when we encourage others, it makes us happy. A right word spoken at the right time is one of the most valuable gifts we can give anyone. We always need encouragement, but there are times in all of our lives when it is a vital need. Those who are discerning will be able to sense when a person deeply needs encouragement.

I have, at times, felt I should text someone or call with an encouragement only to be told in response, "You have no idea how much I needed that." It may have been someone I rarely see or talk with, but God put that person on my heart in such a way that I felt compelled to contact them. I have even had people go so far as to say, "What you just said made my day," or, "When you said that, it changed my life." Hearing comments such as these should tell us plainly that words of encouragement are extremely important and powerful. I am sure the same thing happens to you, too. The important question is, do you listen and take action, or do you simply ignore the prompting from God? Focus on using your words in positive ways, and you won't have to work so hard at not speaking negatively.

LOVE CORRECTION

Proverbs 15 includes five references to correction and discipline, which, as we know, are primary themes of the Book of Proverbs. It is interesting to me that many things Proverbs encourages us to love are things we don't even like, let alone love. No wonder Solomon mentions them over and over. I am sure he does this hoping that we will eventually realize how important they are. Do you love correction? If so, you are among the few who do. A person must be very secure and confident in order to love and gladly receive correction.

One reason we struggle to receive correction, I think, is that we view it improperly. We typically see it as pointing out something wrong about ourselves, and we don't like for other people to notice or mention our flaws. But I say that correction is simply right direction, not an accusation of inferiority or incompetence.

Our team at Joyce Meyer Ministries includes many creative people. They design and package resource covers, magazines, television shows, radio shows, and product advertisements, and they play many other valuable roles in our organization. Sometimes I don't like a design, and I ask them to change it. In those situations, some people have had their feelings hurt and started defending their work. I have shared that there is nothing wrong with their work, but that it simply is not what I want. I have gone on to say that I am not *correcting* them, but *directing* them so they will know how to give me what I want in the future. Some creative people in the past have wanted to give me what *they* like, not what *I* like—and that is where the mistake lies. A person may do something that is very good but still does not meet our specific need or even accomplish what they were hired to do.

Over the course of almost forty years, we have had two or three people who have not been able to stay with us because they simply could not take correction of any kind. That is sad. Now, our creative team is wonderful and they frequently provide designs that are even better than what I think I want. On the few occasions when they don't, I am glad to report that they are very cooperative and agreeable to work with.

Anyone who is employed by an organization should always work to give the employer what they want. That's what they are hired to do. People who work for others may eventually be able to open their own businesses, but as long as they work for someone else, they are getting paid to please the person or organization that compensates them.

Anyone who must always be right in order to be happy will have great difficulty getting through life. I believe that if we know our value in Christ and are confident and secure in Him, we can learn to love correction and receive it as a gift from God.

Some people overcorrect others or correct them using harsh tones. This can break a person's spirit, and it is wrong to treat someone that way. When people find something to correct about almost everything and everyone they encounter, that usually means something is wrong with their attitude and they need to be corrected themselves. Jesus says in Matthew 7 that we are to take the plank out of our own eye and then we can see clearly how to take the speck out of another's eye (vv. 3–5). Another way of communicating this principle would be, "Don't try to correct anyone else unless you are willing to be corrected when you need to be."

Loving correction is as challenging as staying calm and gentle when someone is speaking to you in an angry way. It is not easy, but it must be very important, because it is one of the main subjects covered in the Book of Proverbs.

The wise person loves correction. The wise person also knows how and when to give correction in ways that help others receive it well. We can learn to serve correction covered in sugar, meaning that we can encourage people first about all the things they do right and then mention the one thing we would like them to change.

Let me encourage you to think first, before offering correction. In addition, pray about the right way to approach correction, and God will give you grace to do it effectively and graciously. Also, let us all pray that we can learn to love and appreciate correction when someone offers it in a spirit of love.

PROVERBS 16

Proverbs 16 includes three references to the fact that people often make their own plans without consulting the Lord, who is ultimately in control (vv. 1, 9, 25). Proverbs 16:1 and 16:9 make clear that only the Lord knows what we should do and where we should go, while verse 25 warns us that the way that may seem right leads to a negative outcome.

> To humans belong the plans of the heart, but from the Lord comes the proper answer of the tongue.
>
> Proverbs 16:1

> In their hearts humans plan their course, but the Lord establishes their steps.
>
> Proverbs 16:9

> There is a way that appears to be right, but in the end it leads to death.
>
> Proverbs 16:25

Have you ever asked someone a question and heard an answer beginning with "Well, off the top of my head, I think…" What they mean is that they are about to give you their opinion or advice, without putting much thought into it. The worst advice we can get is advice that comes off of the top of someone's head. We have learned already that wisdom must be waited on and secured before we offer opinions or take action. When we consider how to live our lives, we don't want input from people who do not seek wisdom and thoroughly consider the insights they offer us. If we are sincere about wanting good, solid input, we also do not want people simply to say, "Well, what do you want to do?" The question should not be "What do I want to do?" but "Lord, what do You want me to do?" Proverbs 16:3 says, "Commit to the Lord whatever you do, and he will establish your plans."

There are times when we don't understand what is happening in our lives. We are confused about the direction in which we are going because it isn't what we planned. However, we should be thankful when we see the folly of our plans, because if we trust in God, He will intervene on our behalf and arrange our circumstances so that they will be much better than our plans would have been. I have learned over the years that when I pray for something that God's Word does not specifically mention, I always add, "And Lord, please don't give it to me if it is not Your will." Experience has taught me that getting my way is a mistake if what I want doesn't agree with what God wants. Let's remember the advice

of King Solomon and acknowledge God in all of our ways so
He will direct our paths (Proverbs 3:6).

At times you may find yourself with no sense of what
God would have you do in a situation. When you truly
believe God has not given you
direction in a matter, I believe
that it is fine to make your own
plans. But always submit your
plans to God and be ready to
change directions if He leads
you to do so.

> *Do you try to make your own plans and ask God to bless them, or do you make a habit of submitting your plans to Him?*

LET'S GO DEEPER

"All a person's ways seem pure to them, but motives are
weighed by the Lord" (v. 2). Anytime I teach on the subject
of motives at a conference, the room becomes almost silent.
Our motives are not about *what* we do, but *why* we do it.
What we are doing is easy to see, but our motives are hidden
deep in our hearts. In Jesus' Sermon on the Mount, motives
are among the topics He addresses. He says to be careful not
to practice good deeds in front of others so they will see them
and be impressed. He encourages good deeds, but the motive
must always be to help, not to be noticed or admired. He also
says that those who do good in order to be seen or admired
will have no reward from God (Matthew 6:1). He makes a
similar comment about giving to the needy and instructs that
we should not let our left hand know what our right hand

is doing (Matthew 6:2–3). In this instruction, I believe He is teaching us not to think excessively about the good works we have done, because it would lead to pride. Proverbs 16:5 teaches us that those who are proud in heart are "exceedingly offensive to the Lord" (AMP); therefore, we should seek humility. Jesus also says that we should not pray publicly because we hope others will see and hear us (Matthew 6:5–6). He delights in our prayers, but not if they are motivated by a desire to be seen and admired.

I doubt we will be aware of why we do good or helpful deeds without taking time to truly think about it. Jeremiah said that a person's heart is deceitful above all else, and asks who can know their own heart and mind (Jeremiah 17:9). God, of course, does know our hearts and the motives for everything we do. But in order for us to know our hearts and motives, we must look beyond what we do to why we do it. Being willing to face the truth is the key to uncovering true motives. Anything we do that could be considered a good deed should be done in obedience to God and in an effort to help others, not to be noticed or praised. The fleshly nature loves and craves attention and credit for doing anything that is "good," but God doesn't consider any work good unless the motive behind it is pure.

I believe it is wise to have a meeting with yourself occasionally for the purpose of examining your works and your heart to make sure your motives are pure. You won't learn to examine your motives by rushing through life. You will learn to do it only as you slow down and wait on God to reveal them to you.

ADVICE FOR LEADERS

Proverbs 16 includes several verses addressed to kings, commenting on what their behavior should be. We read that the king's mouth "does not betray justice" (v. 10). He detests wrongdoing, and his "throne is established through righteousness" (v. 12). He takes pleasure in "honest lips" and values "the one who speaks what is right" (v. 13). "A king's wrath is a messenger of death, but the wise will appease it" (v. 14), and a king's favor is like a spring rain (v. 15), which is a blessing.

We can compare a king to a leader. He leads others, and people watch him so they can learn how to do things properly. A wise man or woman does as the king (leader) desires, because to do otherwise could mean the loss of a position. When leaders are honored and obeyed, their favor is abundant toward those who respect and follow them. But to be rebellious is foolish, because rebellion is a serious sin (1 Samuel 15:23).

I think most of us would agree that more and more people today are rebellious toward any kind of authority. We find very few who know the importance of submitting to authority with a good attitude. God sets up lines of authority not simply so that one person can rule over everyone else, but to establish and maintain peace and order.

I think it is important for me to clarify that we should not submit to anyone's authority if what that person tells us to do would be sinful. I fear that the true spiritual doctrine regarding submission to authority has been all but lost, but we can still find it throughout God's Word.

Leaders have great privileges, but they also have great responsibilities. They should not take leadership positions if they are not also willing to take the responsibilities that go along with them. This is doubly true for spiritual leaders. They represent God, and their actions should reflect what He would do in every situation. One of their responsibilities is to treat those under their authority with respect, gentleness, and love, just as Christ would. Usually, if a leader treats people justly, they are happy to submit to his or her authority. This is generally true, but not always, because some people simply have a rebellious attitude and do not want to take direction from anyone, including God.

BEWARE OF GOSSIP

"A perverse person stirs up conflict, and a gossip separates close friends" (v. 28). Gossip is dangerous, and we should not participate in it. Because of the sin nature that was in us before we were born again, gossip is tempting. Some people love to know a secret that is not complimentary about someone else and to spread it quickly. If those who hear it spread it to others and that process repeats itself several times, the person who started it due to lack of discretion has stirred up a storm with a few words.

If you have ever been the victim of vicious gossip, you

know how painful it can be. When rumors are spread, usually without facts to substantiate them, an innocent person's reputation can be destroyed. Social media today has become a common place for people to give their opinions on many things about which they actually know nothing. But sadly, people who read what they say often believe it. We should never believe a bad report about anyone without the confirmation of two or three reliable witnesses (2 Corinthians 13:1).

Several months ago, a woman I know called me and began telling me that a friend of mine had done some terrible things. My immediate response was, "I'm sorry, but I just don't believe that." She went on to tell me who had given her the information and to say that the person who shared the story with her supposedly had firsthand knowledge of it.

My answer was still that I did not believe it, but would call the person being accused and ask her outright if she was guilty of these things. I made a phone call and within a few minutes knew I had been correct; the accused person was innocent. She explained to me what had really happened, and it was nothing like what had been reported to me. That is the danger of gossip: Each person who hears and repeats it usually adds a little to it or changes it slightly. Before long, the story is completely devoid of truth.

When a piece of gossip comes your way, make sure it stops with you. Don't ever spread it. More importantly, don't ever start it.

PATIENCE, PLEASE

"Better a patient person than a warrior, one with self-control than one who takes a city" (v. 32). This scripture speaks of the power of patience and self-control. A patient person is better than a warrior who can capture an entire city. Just think about what this is saying.

Impatience has been my greatest weakness—and probably to some degree it still is. I will admit that I simply do not like waiting on things. Impatient people are often quick to verbally express how they feel or blame someone who isn't moving at their desired pace.

I do better waiting on God than waiting on people. Maybe I have learned that God isn't going to hurry no matter what I do, but I keep hoping that people will pick up the pace. God is working with me, and I trust that, little by little, He is changing me. But I just want to admit here that patience is not easy for

How patient and self-controlled are you?

me. The first step toward freedom is admitting that you have a problem, so if you are also impatient, you can join me in learning to remain peaceful and patient in all situations.

Over the years I have developed a lot of patience, but I don't want to be satisfied with being patient most of the time. I want to be patient all the time, as Jesus is.

I pray that by now you are seeing how practical the Book of Proverbs is and how important studying it is to the Christian life. It gives us hundreds of life lessons that will help us serve God better and enjoy life more.

PROVERBS 17

Proverbs 17 has eight references to the fool (a morally deficient person) or the foolish (vv. 7, 10, 12, 16, 21, 24, 25, 28). A fool is the exact opposite of a wise person. Because this chapter refers to the fool so many times, it is prudent for us to take a close look at how a foolish person behaves.

Many of the references we find in Proverbs to fools have something to say about their speech and how they use their words. We have already learned that the fool speaks rashly and talks too much. Plato observed, "Wise men speak because they have something to say, fools because they have to say something." A quotation that has been around for generations and attributed in various forms to various people, including Mark Twain, Abraham Lincoln, and even Confucius, says, "It is better to keep your mouth closed and let people think you are a fool than to open it and remove all doubt." No matter who said this originally, it's true!

Although we have read that wisdom cries out in the streets (Proverbs 1:20–21), we know from experience that wisdom also often speaks softly. That is not the case with foolishness; it screams long and loud. The enemy has a way of making evil alluring, tempting, and appealing. Temptation never focuses on a future outcome but lives for the moment, urging people to pursue instant gratification. Satan is the great deceiver; he is very crafty, and we must be on our guard concerning him and his lies. He continually bombards our minds with lies and foolish, useless thoughts that demand our attention and try to wear down our defenses against those lies. Every action eventually has a corresponding outcome, and the foolish act without giving thought to ultimate consequences. The wise, however, keep the end results of their behavior in mind.

Since we have learned that moral deficiency describes foolishness, we know that foolish people have no interest in obeying God, generally speaking. Or they may be partially committed to God, but not committed to Him wholeheartedly, as He desires us to be. They imagine they can live as fools and still have a blessed life, but that is impossible.

We make a big mistake if we think that temptation attacks only those who are already sinning. If they should repent of their sin and try to do what is right, Proverbs 9:15 says that folly calls to those who are making their paths straight. Foolishness does not want people to walk a straight or narrow path, and the devil hates and tries to hinder any kind of progress in the right direction. The apostle Paul says that when he tried to do good, evil always came (Romans 7:21). Satan does all he can to keep us from loving, obeying, and serving God.

After forty-five years of diligently studying God's Word, I can say that the main lesson I see over and over has never changed: If we do as God instructs, we will live a blessed and enjoyable life, but if we disobey Him, we experience misery of every kind.

OBEDIENCE VERSUS DISOBEDIENCE

At times we may think that obeying God in certain areas of our lives is simply too hard. Actually, even when obedience is difficult in the beginning, disobedience ends up being much harder in the long run. Deuteronomy 30:11–14 teaches us that obeying God's commands is not too hard for us: "The word is very near you; it is in your mouth and in your heart so you may obey it" (v. 14). If we confess God's Word with our mouth and meditate on it in our hearts and minds, we will be able to obey it. Meditation, or the habit of thinking about something over and over again, renews our minds and allows them to grasp the principles we are thinking about. Regularly confessing or speaking aloud the truths of God's Word has the same effect. Meditation and confession are effective in both positive and negative ways. They work for good or for evil.

If I meditate on and talk about something unjust that someone has done to me, it will only make me more and more determined to be angry with that person and want revenge.

> Do you make a habit of meditating on God's Word?

However, if I think about forgiving that individual while remembering that I frequently need forgiveness myself, it will enable me to let go of the offense and continue showing God's love to them. Our thoughts and words prepare us to take action.

Obedience may be challenging for a little while, especially

if we have to sacrifice something in order to obey, but the results of disobedience can hurt us for a lifetime.

THE EVEN-TEMPERED

Proverbs 17 reminds us of the importance of peace and the danger of strife, quarrels, offenses, and anger. Proverbs 17:1 says, "Better a dry crust with peace and quiet than a house full of feasting, with strife." This teaches us that we would be better off to have few possessions and even very little to eat with peace and quiet, rather than having everything money could provide and living in an atmosphere of strife. Many people live in constant strife, trying to obtain material possessions. In the process, they lose the qualities of life that are most important, such as peace and joy, a close relationship with God, and loving relationships with family and friends.

Many families are filled with strife, anger, and offense simply because one or both parents are so busy trying to make a lot of money that they are rarely home and do not take time to attend sports events, recitals, or other activities in which their children are involved. They do not make the effort to talk to or really listen to their sons and daughters, and although they say they love each other, they do not take time to do anything special for their spouses or spend quality time with them. When this happens, it often leaves a root of bitterness in the children, which may affect them adversely for the rest of their lives. One thing is for sure: At the end of their lives, people who pursue money and material goods with excessive intensity won't be asking for their bank balance. They will want family to be with them and care about them. If parents such as the ones I have described do not invest in their children throughout their lives, the children may not be around when the parents pass away.

Proverbs 17:9 says, "Whoever would foster love covers over an offense, but whoever repeats the matter separates close friends." Loving God and loving people is our highest call, and it is something we need to prioritize in our lives. Love always forgives. Love covers offenses; it doesn't expose them. First Peter 4:8 says: "Above all, love each other deeply, because love covers over a multitude of sins."

We can better understand the idea of covering sin through the example of an incident involving Noah and his sons. We read in Genesis 8–9 that after the ark had settled and the waters had receded to the point that Noah and his family could walk out on dry ground, Noah planted a vineyard. Later, he made wine from the grapes he grew and drank enough to get drunk. He ended up lying naked in his tent. Noah's son, Ham, saw his father's nakedness and told his two brothers, Shem and Japheth. Shem and Japheth walked backward into their father's tent, carrying a blanket, and covered their father's nakedness with it. When Noah awoke and realized what had happened, he cursed Ham, but he blessed Shem and Japheth.

Ham was foolish. He didn't cover his father's mistake but quickly went and told his brothers about it. The brothers, in contrast, were wise and covered their father.

I believe there is tremendous power in covering an offense

and quickly forgiving those who hurt us. It is important to love at all times, because God is love (1 John 4:8). When we abide in love, we abide in God (1 John 4:16).

DROP IT!

"Starting a quarrel is like breaching a dam; so drop the matter before a dispute breaks out" (v. 14). Jesus speaks of this same principle in Mark 11:25: "Whenever you stand praying, if you have anything against anyone, forgive him and let it drop (leave it, let it go), in order that your Father Who is in heaven may also forgive you your [own] failings and shortcomings and let them drop" (AMPC).

Many years ago, before I understood the importance of forgiveness, when I became angry with Dave I would bring up the supposed offense over and over again. He would often ask, "Can't you just drop it?" At the time, I didn't know how to drop it, but since I have learned how much damage strife, bickering, arguing, and harboring offense can cause, I drop a contentious matter quickly, as though it is a poison that I don't want to touch me.

Proverbs 17:27 says, "The one who has knowledge uses words with restraint, and whoever has understanding is even-tempered." Strife, anger, and offense are often connected to words spoken when they should have been left unsaid. How many times do our feelings get hurt because of something that someone has said to us? Probably more often than we realize.

ADDITIONAL WISDOM FROM
PROVERBS 17

Proverbs 17 makes many other wise points. Space doesn't allow me to expound on each one of them. However, I will mention some of them.

- We are reminded to be prudent because the prudent person will lead wisely in family matters (v. 2).
- Solomon lets us know that as silver and gold are tested in fire to find and remove any impurities, God also tests His people (v. 3). He may allow us to be in an uncomfortable place or experience difficulties as tests of our faith. It is important to love God and obey Him in hard times, not just in good times.
- One rebuke impresses a discerning person more than a hundred lashes impresses a fool (v. 10). Wise and discerning people learn to appreciate words of rebuke and correction, because they know such words will make them better and help them grow.
- Also, a true friend loves at all times, even in adversity (v. 17). If you have friends who are there for you only when you're up but cannot be found when you are down, they are not true friends. In Jesus, we have a friend who sticks closer than a brother (Proverbs 18:24).
- Proverbs 17 also includes several more references to the mouth and the power of words (vv. 4, 7, 20, 27, 28).

I will mention one more principle from this chapter, because it is very important: "A cheerful heart is good medicine, but a crushed spirit dries up the bones" (v. 22). I cannot encourage you strongly enough: Be happy, laugh often, and let the joy of the Lord be your strength (Nehemiah 8:10). We cannot always find joy in our circumstances, but simply thinking about all the amazing things God has done for us in Christ is enough to keep us joyful day after day.

PROVERBS 18

Most of us love to give advice. But most people don't want advice unless they specifically request it. Even then, they don't always want it unless it agrees with what they already want to do. Proverbs 18:2 says that fools "delight in airing their own opinions." We should all learn to offer our opinions sparingly.

Many offenses and much strife come from voicing unsolicited opinions. Why do we find such delight in sharing our opinions? I think it is a matter of pride; we want others to think we have knowledge. Sometimes we want them to think we know more than we do. But if we are honest, we will admit that often we give opinions about things we don't really know much about. We want people to do what we think we would do if we were in their situation. But how can we possibly know what we would do in a situation in which we have never found ourselves?

Opinions are usually birthed from judgment. Romans 14:4 says, "Who are you to judge someone else's servant?" Each of us is a servant of God, and He alone has the right to judge us.

In our pride we may think that if we don't own a certain item, others don't need it, either. Let's say that a friend purchases a new, rather expensive car, and you say to another friend, "I don't think she needs such an expensive car." But you really don't know what she needs or what God has given her permission to purchase. Statements such as these are typically rooted in jealousy, not wisdom. They may represent what we think, but really, the situation is none of our business. In addition, the day may come when you will purchase a car even more expensive than the one you judged someone else for buying. "I would never do that" is most often a foolish statement because we frequently end up doing what we said we would never do.

> Make it your ambition to lead a quiet life: You should
> mind your own business and work with your hands.
> 1 Thessalonians 4:11

Just think about how much better the world would be if people would stop offering opinions about things that are none of their business. I will admit that at one time I was a very nosy person. I wanted to know what was going on in everyone's life, and I had an abundance of opinions about their choices. Thankfully, God has patiently taught me how foolish it is to behave that way. Although I have not arrived at the place of perfection in this area, I have come a long way. I often have to say to myself, "Joyce, that is none of your business!"

Are you often tempted to get involved in situations that are none of your business, and if so, do you resist those temptations?

HUMILITY BRINGS HONOR

"Before a downfall the heart is haughty, but humility comes before honor" (v. 12). People who walk in humility are not quick to give opinions or advice. They prefer to keep quiet rather than speak whenever they feel like saying something without direction from God. First Peter 5:6 says that if we humble ourselves "under God's mighty hand," He will lift us up at the appropriate time. If we have knowledge about a certain situation and God wants us to share it, He can easily arrange for that. If not, we should be satisfied to be quiet.

We may blame trouble or a downfall in our lives on many things, but Scripture teaches us that pride always comes before destruction (Proverbs 16:18). We must purposefully avoid pride and pray that God will help us stay humble.

The flesh craves attention, but giving the flesh what it wants only feeds and strengthens it. Every time you deny the flesh, it becomes weaker and you become stronger. Keeping your opinions to yourself, unless they affirm or encourage people, is one way to practice humility on a daily basis.

THE POWER OF LIFE AND DEATH

In Proverbs 18, we see another eight references to the mouth and the words we speak. I am absolutely amazed at the number of references to this one subject in Proverbs, and I am convinced that if the Holy Spirit gives so much attention to it in Scripture, it must be very important. We find teaching about the mouth in Proverbs 18: 4, 6, 7, 8, 13, 17, 20, and 21. I would like us to look closely at three of these verses, Proverbs 18:13 and Proverbs 18:20–21.

Proverbs 18:13 says, "To answer before listening—that is folly and shame." I have to admit that sometimes I think about what I will say in response to what someone else is saying before he or she finishes speaking. But how can we offer an appropriate response unless we have heard and thought about what has been said? We can't! We may give some type of answer because dispensing advice and answers makes us feel important. But if that advice is wrong, we only prove our foolishness. Sometimes the best answer is, "I don't know" or "Let me think about it before I give you an answer."

I consider Proverbs 18:20–21 two of the Bible's strongest verses about the power of words.

> From the fruit of their mouth a person's stomach is filled; with the harvest of their lips they are satisfied. The tongue has the power of life and death, and those who love it will eat its fruit.
>
> Proverbs 18:20–21

Words are so powerful that they can actually minister (impart) life or death. If we believe this, we will be very careful about what we say. One kind word can change someone's entire day. I once read that words are free, but the way we use them may cost us. Angry, belittling words spoken to a child by a parent may stay with that child for a lifetime and may even kill a hope or a dream inside that child's heart. Perhaps we should taste our words before we spit them out.

Not only do our words affect those who are listening, they also affect us. Proverbs 18:21 actually says that we eat our words. In other words, we not only speak words, but we also hear them, and they influence us on the inside, ministering life or death to us. If you are a frequent complainer, you have less joy than a person who is thankful—and that ministers death. If you compliment people frequently, it increases your joy, which ministers life.

Proverbs 18:20 says that there is a harvest from our lips. We reap the seeds we sow, and words are definitely seeds. They produce a harvest, and we should be wise enough to sow according to what we hope to reap. No one can plant apple seeds and reap oranges.

Words are powerful, whether they are spoken to someone or simply spoken into the atmosphere around us. I believe strongly in confessing God's Word aloud. The definition of *confess* that I like to use is "to say the same as." So when we confess God's Word, we are saying the same things God says, and this is extremely powerful. I have even written a book called *The Secret Power of Speaking God's Word*, which teaches how to confess His Word and includes many Scripture confessions that have the power to change your life.

I urge you to speak what God speaks. By doing so you put yourself into agreement with Him, and you will experience His good will in your life. If God says He loves you, then you say that God loves you. You would not necessarily say this to another person, but confessing it in the privacy of your home or while driving in your car is extremely powerful. Say that God surrounds you with favor, and expect to see His favor manifest in your life, because that is what His Word says. Speaking the Word aloud helps renew your mind and increases your faith. Keep your mind and mouth focused on good things from God's Word, and there will be no room for the enemy to fill your thoughts and words with things that bring harm and make you unhappy.

> Keep this Book of the Law always on your lips; meditate on it day and night, so that you may be careful to do everything written in it. Then you will be prosperous and successful.
>
> Joshua 1:8

In Psalm 19:14, David asks God to make the words of his mouth and the meditation of his heart acceptable to Him. This is an excellent example for us to follow.

We cannot tame the tongue simply by trying hard to do so. We need a lot of help from God in order to speak the way He wants us to speak. Therefore, this is an area that is worth praying about daily, or perhaps several times a day. Lean and rely on God, and you will steadily improve.

Let me encourage you to read through Proverbs and highlight every Scripture verse on words, the lips, and the tongue. If you do this, then when you need a refresher course, you can look at the highlighted areas and be strengthened in

God's will concerning this important area. When you make mistakes don't feel condemned, just ask for forgiveness and begin again.

Choosing our words wisely is definitely an area in which slowing down our pace in life will help us. If we think about what we are going to say before saying it, we will speak wisdom instead of foolishness, God will be honored, and our lives will benefit greatly.

PROVERBS 19

Proverbs 19 gives us a great deal of good advice, which, if followed, will open the door to blessings in our lives. Verse 2 says, "Desire without knowledge is not good" and "hasty feet miss the way!" We all have desires, but not everything we want is best for us to have. Trusting God involves believing that if we don't get what we want, God knows it would not be best for us and withholds it because He has something better in mind. Sometimes what we desire is God's will, but the timing isn't right for us to have it, so we need to wait. Proverbs 19:21 affirms this, saying, "Many are the plans in a person's heart, but it is the Lord's purpose that prevails."

> *Are you willing to trust God's timing in your life?*

You can ask God for anything, but let me encourage you not to be upset if you don't get what you request. Just trust Him and stay peaceful. James writes, "You do not have because you do not ask God" (James 4:2). But sometimes we ask and don't receive, and that may be because we have asked "with wrong motives" (James 4:3).

Finding ways to get something that isn't God's will for us is a mistake, because it will do nothing but cause trouble. Let's say that you really want to take a vacation with some friends who invite you to an oceanside resort. You ask God for the extra money to be able to go. But the money never comes, so you go anyway and put the expenses on a credit card. You enjoy yourself, but then the credit card bill arrives, and you cannot pay all of what you charged, so you make the minimum payment. This goes on for several months. You soon find yourself frustrated because the interest charged to your account keeps adding up as long as you pay only the minimum amount due instead of the full balance. Even after making payments for months, your balance never seems to go down very much. After a while, you wish you had never taken the vacation. But it is too late, and you're stuck with the debt. You're in a difficult situation because you forced your plan instead of waiting and saving in order to take the vacation without going into debt.

Proverbs tells us that the borrower is the servant of the lender (Proverbs 22:7), so we should stay out of debt as much as possible. Since we know that debt is unwise and a vacation is not something a person must have right away, what we should do is clear. But when we want something strongly, we often override wisdom and do as we please—and we end up regretting it later.

We need to learn how to discern between when God is opening a door for us and when we are pushing a door open ourselves. We can make some things happen, but doing so is not always wise. The psalmist says, "Unless the Lord builds the house, the builders labor in vain" (Psalm 127:1). In other words, we can work hard to build or do something, but unless

God is in it, all of that effort turns out to be useless. The fact that we *can* do something does not mean it is the right thing to do. When I pray for something and I am not sure about it, I always ask the Lord not to give it to me if it isn't right for me. I don't want what He doesn't want me to have, because I have learned the hard way that it will only steal my peace and cause problems I would rather not have to face.

The more important a decision is, the more important it is to take your time and do your best to discern God's will before taking action. If I don't know what God wants me to do, I usually take one step forward to see if it works. If it does, only then do I take a second step. If that works, I take the next step, and so on. God doesn't give us a blueprint for our entire lives. He guides us one step at a time. Don't be afraid to take that first step, but if it doesn't work, don't be afraid to step back, either.

HOW TO TREAT THOSE WHO ARE POOR

"Wealth attracts many friends, but even the closest friend of the poor person deserts them" (v. 4). "The poor are shunned by all their relatives—how much more do their friends avoid them! Though the poor pursue them with pleading, they are nowhere to be found" (v. 7).

These verses indicate that the poor are often shunned and devalued, but God teaches us in His Word to love and help them.

Whoever is kind to the poor lends to the Lord, and he
will reward them for what they have done.

Proverbs 19:17

God seems to have a special place in His heart for the poor,
the needy, widows, and orphans. He tells us to stand up for
their rights and to give to them and help them. Joyce Meyer
Ministries has an outreach called Hand of Hope. Through it,
we are blessed to be able to help many people who are hurting and need help, not only spiritually but also in practical
ways. I believe that preaching the gospel and helping people
in need go hand in hand. Sometimes people are hurting so
much that they cannot hear a message about God, but if you
show them that God loves them by helping them unconditionally, then they want to hear what you have to say. People
who are starving may struggle to believe that God loves them,
but if you feed them, their hearts are more open to hearing
the gospel.

I believe that all of us who call ourselves Christians
should help the poor. If you don't know anyone who is strug-
gling financially, then find the shelters in your city that help
the homeless, the hungry, and the needy. Donate money or
volunteer your time to help them. Every church should have
programs geared toward helping the poor, because it is a
work of God. Giving financially to those churches and ministries is a way to help people in need.

When you have a personal need, you may be tempted
to isolate and feel sorry for yourself, but the wise course of
action is to "trust in the Lord and do good" (Psalm 37:3).

Get involved in helping others, because reaching out to help someone is a way of sowing seed for the harvest you need. I am continually amazed that when I have a problem and cannot help myself, God will enable me to help someone else. This is because He wants us to reach *out*, not *in*. As we reach out to others, God will reach into our lives and help us.

We are to open our hands wide to the poor (Deuteronomy 15:11). God has given us hearts of compassion, and we can either open them or close them.

> If anyone has material possessions and sees a brother or sister in need but has no pity on them, how can the love of God be in that person? Dear children, let us not love with words or speech but with actions and in truth.
>
> 1 John 3:17–18

Love is a living thing. It must be active rather than stagnant. Just as a pool of water that has no movement will become stagnant, love will do the same without fresh inflow and outflow. God pours His love into us, and He wants us to let it flow through us to others. Love can be shown in many ways. Helping the poor and treating them with respect is one important way to demonstrate it.

Sacrificing to help those in need says a lot about our character. A generous person is a happy person. Paul tells us, "Be mindful to be a blessing, especially to those of the household of faith" (Galatians 6:10 AMPC). In other words, we should keep our minds full of ways we can bless others.

Why would a poor person's friends and relatives desert him, as Proverbs 19:4, 7 says? I can think of a few reasons. They might be embarrassed to be seen with a poor person. Or perhaps they realize that the needy person cannot do anything for them, so they don't want to spend their time with him or her. That, of course, is a selfish attitude and not one that has God's approval. Perhaps they feel like the poor person could help himself or herself if they really wanted to. That may be true in some cases, but not in all of them. The Bible says that "mercy triumphs over judgment" (James 2:13), so I prefer to go with mercy and let God show me if I

Are you helping the poor?

am not doing as He desires. There are circumstances under which giving to the poor simply enables them to stay poor, but most of the time that is not the case. We should care enough to at least look into the situation to discern what needs to be done.

We cannot single-handedly eliminate poverty, but all of us can help someone. If every Christian simply helps one person, it will make a huge difference. Just put yourself in the place of someone sleeping on the street or in an abandoned building, and then imagine you are twelve years old, all alone and doing this night after night. This happens in every city and nation, and it is indeed tragic. We may not be able to do everything, but we must refuse to do nothing.

PROVERBS 20

Proverbs 20 opens with an observation about the effects of alcohol, saying, "Wine is a mocker and beer a brawler; whoever is led astray by them is not wise" (v. 1). Alcohol should be consumed sparingly, because those who are excessive with it will be led astray by it and not behave wisely. If a person cannot use moderation in drinking alcohol, they are better off avoiding it entirely. Some people believe that drinking any kind of alcohol is wrong, and in that case, they should follow their conscience.

Paul told Timothy to drink a little wine for the sake of his stomach (1 Timothy 5:23), and he told deacons and elders that they should not drink too much wine (1 Timothy 3:8). He also said not to get drunk with wine, but to be filled with the Holy Spirit (Ephesians 5:18). I cannot find a scripture to support forbidding the drinking of wine. However, alcohol has caused problems for many people, and I can certainly understand why many people are entirely against drinking alcohol. There are also a number of scriptures directing certain individuals not to drink strong drink of any kind. John the Baptist, for example, was forbidden wine or strong drink (Luke 1:15), as was Samson in the Old Testament (Judges

13:7). Yet Jesus drank wine, and His first miracle was to turn water into wine at a wedding (John 2:1–10).

The Bible seems to make cases for both drinking in moderation and not drinking wine or strong drink at all, so each individual must follow their own convictions in this matter and not judge those who hold different convictions. Be led by the Holy Spirit and do as God leads you.

PREPARING FOR HARVEST

The only way to prepare for harvest is to work hard during plowing and seed-sowing seasons. Proverbs 20 warns against laziness, as do many other chapters in Proverbs. It says that lazy people (sluggards) "do not plow in season; so at harvest time they look but find nothing" (v. 4). It also says if you love to sleep you will be poor, but if you stay awake "you will have food to spare" (v. 13). You may remember that Proverbs 19 also addresses laziness. Proverbs 19:24 says, "A sluggard buries his hand in the dish; he will not even bring it back to his mouth!" This sounds about as lazy as anyone could possibly be! Proverbs 19:15 says, "Laziness brings on deep sleep, and the shiftless go hungry." God created us to work as well as to rest, and those who don't work (unless they are unable to do so for medical reasons) are not fulfilled and satisfied.

These scriptures help us clearly see that laziness produces nothing good in our lives. I find that doing my work early in the day is best for me. Sometimes, if I wait too long to get started, the work becomes something I simply don't want to do, and I may end up putting it off. Other people may work better in the evenings. I encourage you to be thoughtful and intentional about what you need to accomplish each day, find your most productive hours during each day, and make the most of them as opposed to putting off tasks and risking never accomplishing them.

Today I have a choice to make: I can work out at the gym, or I can wait until tomorrow. I know that if I work out today, when I wake up tomorrow, I will be glad I've already completed this important activity. But I've had to have a few conversations with myself in order to finally make the commitment to go today. I am using wisdom and doing today what I will be happy with tomorrow. To ensure that I don't back out of going to the gym today, I have called and arranged for someone to go with me, knowing that if I have a commitment to another person, I will definitely go. I am out of town right now, so I have no set days to exercise and no appointments with a trainer, so it is up to me to discipline myself.

Discipline usually requires a firm decision. Hebrews 12:11 teaches us that no discipline seems joyous when we are in the midst of it, but later on, discipline yields peace. One thing that helped me make up my mind to work out today was knowing from experience that sitting and writing this book all day with no physical exercise will make me very tired. Exercise and activity actually give us energy if we balance them with appropriate rest. I didn't think it would be good to write about the dangers of being lazy while being lazy myself.

The sluggard does what he feels like doing, not what is good for him, but he always pays the price in the end. A few people have everything handed to them without having to work, but very few. Most of us have to invest hard work and energy if we want to enjoy good things in our lives. We have to pay the price now in order to enjoy life later.

One of the first things God did for Adam was to give him a job. He was to tend the garden and be fruitful and multiply (Genesis 1:28; 2:15). God works *through* us, not instead of us. He will always help us, but He also always leaves to us the choice of whether to work or not.

The longer a person is lazy and passive, the harder it is to get going again. The best way to live is to maintain a balance between work and rest. This will help you stay out of trouble. There is nothing wrong with having a do-nothing day, but if every day is a day off, it becomes a problem. I love this old saying: "The more you do, the more you can do, and the less you do, the less you can do."

TRUTH AND HONESTY

Truth and honesty are primary themes of Proverbs. We are not to lie or deceive anyone in any way. Proverbs 20:10 says, "Differing weights and differing measures—the Lord detests them both." In Bible times, people shopped at marketplaces. When they purchased items such as grain, sellers measured it using scales and balances. Sellers could falsify the readings and cheat their customers by using false weights. God says that He detests that kind of behavior. Jesus is the Truth, and Satan is the deceiver, so we can quickly see why truth is so important.

Proverbs 19 also touches on this theme: "A false witness will not go unpunished, and whoever pours out lies will not go free" (Proverbs 19:5). Proverbs 19:9 repeats this, saying, "whoever pours out lies will perish."

Some people talk about little white lies, but there is no such thing. A lie is a lie if there is even a tiny bit of untruth in it. We are to tell the truth even if doing so hurts us or causes us trouble. I once had an employer who wanted me to lie to a customer we were expecting the next day and get the customer to pay more than he owed. I wrestled with the decision all night, because I didn't want to lose my job, but by morning I had decided I had to refuse to do as my employer asked, even if it cost me my job. I spoke with the employer, and initially he was angry. But not only did I not lose my job, a couple of years later I was promoted to a high level of management. All true promotion comes from God (Psalm 75:6–7). If we are honest, God can give us favor with people who ordinarily wouldn't like us at all.

Proverbs 19:22 says that it is "better to be poor than a liar." Part of being honest and truthful is doing what we tell people we will do. If you tell someone you will help them with a project, then show up to help with a good attitude. Arrive at your appointments on time unless you have an emergency, and if that is the case, at least communicate that you will be late and explain why.

Being dishonest has become so commonplace in our society these days that if we are not careful, we can compromise to the point that eventually we don't even know we are doing it. God calls us to a high standard. Jesus says, "For everyone to whom much is given, from him much will be required" (Luke 12:48 NKJV). The Lord recently reminded me of this scripture when I wanted to do something that He wasn't giving me permission to do, even though other people I knew were doing it. I murmured to Him about it, and He reminded me of Luke 12:48. He even confirmed it by putting this scripture in front of me the next day from an entirely random source.

There are times when we want God to do a lot for us, but we are not willing to sacrifice what He may ask us to sacrifice. We are in the world, but we are not allowed to behave as the world behaves (John 17:13–16). I reached into my purse the other day to pay for something at a store and found a kitchen fork. It was not a fork from my house, so that meant I somehow put or dropped it into my purse at a restaurant where I had eaten several days earlier. Dave asked me if I would return the fork, and at first I said no. I explained that taking it back would require me to make a special trip to the restaurant, that I didn't want to be embarrassed, and that the restaurant had plenty of forks. On and on my excuses

> *Can you say that you are completely honest and always keep your word?*

went. Then Dave reminded me that I teach people that if they are given too much change at a store to be sure to give back the extra money. I knew then that I had to return the fork. Ouch! I was caught by my own preaching.

I still don't know how that fork got into my purse, but I sure am taking a lot of teasing from family and friends about lifting the silverware!

PROVERBS 21

Proverbs 21 begins by telling us that the king's heart is in the hand of the Lord, and He turns it as He chooses (v. 1). This is good news, because it means that if we trust in God, He will bring justice into our lives. I have written about the time I refused to lie for my employer and not only kept my job but later received a promotion. I believe with all my heart that it was God who changed my employer's mind toward me. He turned that man's heart to give me favor instead of dismissal.

I recommend praying for favor with those who are in authority over you, because even if they intend to do you harm, God can change their hearts toward you. I always thought I had to take care of myself until I learned of this promise and others similar to it in God's Word. Life is much easier and less stressful if we trust God to take care of us instead of pushing and shoving our way through life, trying to make people treat us fairly.

No wisdom, no insight, and no plan can succeed against the Lord (v. 30). No matter what we plan or what anyone else plans, God is ultimately in control.

OBEDIENCE INSTEAD OF SACRIFICE

"To do what is right and just is more acceptable to the Lord than sacrifice" (v. 3). Have you ever disobeyed God and then perhaps given an extra offering, thinking it would make up for your disobedience? In the past, I have done that and similar things. These kinds of sacrifices are not acceptable to the Lord. He wants our obedience, not our works of the flesh trying to pay for our mistakes.

When we sin by not obeying God, there is only one way to be forgiven and justified: through repentance and receiving God's gracious gift of forgiveness. I wasted a lot of years feeling guilty when I did wrong, until God showed me that the guilt was my way of trying to pay for my sins and that He had already done that. We cannot add to the work that Jesus did on the cross. He did a complete job, once and for all. No more sacrifice is needed.

Hebrews 10:11–18 explains why we don't have to work at sacrificing to God for our sins. Jesus' one-time sacrifice on the cross paid for all sin for all time. Thinking about the Hebrew practice in which priests regularly offered the same sacrifices, the apostle Paul writes that these sacrifices "can never take away sins" (Hebrews 10:11). Paul then describes what Jesus, our high priest, has done for us:

But when this priest had offered for all time one sacrifice for sins, he sat down at the right hand of God, and since that time he waits for his enemies to be made his footstool. For by one sacrifice he has made perfect forever those who are being made holy. The Holy Spirit also testifies to us about this. First he says: "This is the covenant I will make with them after that time, says the Lord. I will put my laws in their hearts, and I will write them on their minds." Then he adds: "Their sins and lawless acts I will remember no more." And where these have been forgiven, sacrifice for sin is no longer necessary.

Hebrews 10:12–18

Are you trying to make sacrifices for your sins, and if so, what kind? I can remember sacrificing my joy and enjoyment of life because I thought I was not worthy of it. I sacrificed my peace through continual feelings of guilt. I worked really hard, hoping that God would be pleased with me and accept me. I wore myself out working and working to do something that Jesus had already done. All I needed to do was repent and accept His forgiveness, and that is all you need to do.

When we repent of our sins, we are not merely sorry we sinned. Repentance means that we desire to turn in a completely new direction and become obedient to God. This is a much better plan than sinning and then feeling guilty or trying to work hard to pay for our sins.

Do you continue to suffer with feelings of guilt long after you have repented of your sin?

In 1 Samuel 15, we read that Saul partially obeys God, and then his soldiers make sacrifices for his disobedience. God speaks to him through Samuel the prophet, saying that obedience is better than sacrifice (v. 22). God is not interested in part-time obedience, but He desires for us to follow Him wholeheartedly and do all of His will.

BE EASY TO GET ALONG WITH

Twice in Proverbs 21 Solomon writes that it is better to live in a desert or the corner of a roof than to share a house with a quarrelsome and nagging wife (vv. 9, 19). He also mentions this in Proverbs 25:24 and Proverbs 27:15. Solomon had many wives, so I assume he had experience that caused him to pen these observations. As a woman, I will add that it is also miserable to live with a quarrelsome and nagging husband. Solomon doesn't mention that, so I thought I would!

Although I am a woman, I will admit that in most cases women tend to talk more than men do. The more we talk, the more likely we are to say things we should not say. Using our words to murmur and complain is at the top of the "do not do this" list.

We employ several hundred people at our ministry, and we enjoy what I call our low-maintenance employees. These are people who come to work and do their jobs without constantly finding something to complain about. They are thankful for their jobs, and they have good attitudes when they are asked to do something extra or are inconvenienced for some reason. Complainers

Do you frequently complain?

will always find something to complain about, no matter how positive their circumstances are.

If you are married to a man who goes to work every day, I am sure that after working hard all day and dealing with traffic while trying to get home, the last thing he wants is to walk in the house to hear murmuring, nagging, and complaining. If you do need to discuss something with him, pray first and pick a good time (hint: It's usually not the minute he gets home). Women who stay home and raise families work hard, too, and I doubt that they want

> *Would you consider yourself to be a person who is easy to get along with?*

their husbands to walk through the door complaining about everything at work. The bottom line is that nobody really enjoys listening to continual complaining, murmuring, grumbling, and nagging. Let's decide to be easy to get along with and ask God for what we want and need instead of expecting other people to provide our joy and satisfaction.

GREED VERSUS GIVING

The Bible has much to say about greed and the greedy person. Greedy people are never satisfied. They always want more and more. God's Word says, "The craving of a sluggard will be the death of him, because his hands refuse to work. All day long he craves for more, but the righteous give without sparing" (vv. 25–26). Greedy people focus on getting, but righteous people focus on giving.

Paul thought that greedy people were so dangerous that he instructed believers to not even eat a meal with someone guilty of greed, among other sins (1 Corinthians 5:11). Jesus says, "Watch out! Be on your guard against all kinds of greed; life does not consist in an abundance of possessions" (Luke 12:15). An unbeliever may not know any better, but a believer does. If we know what is right to do and don't do it, then it is sin (James 4:17).

Anyone can fall prey to the spirit of greed, and we should guard against it. One of the best ways I know to avoid it is to be an aggressive giver. When we give cheerfully, God always gives more back than we gave away. But when we are stingy and greedy, we neither prosper nor experience joy and enjoyment of life. Money and possessions have no power in them to give us joy. We may be momentarily happy when we can buy something we want, but the joy does not last very long, and we soon find ourselves wanting something else. The greedy person's life is stolen from them by continual wants and never-ending dissatisfaction.

It may be difficult for a greedy person to give, but generosity is the only antidote to greed. When we get something, we only get a thing that is fleeting and temporary. But when we give, we gain the joy of making someone else happy and we please the Lord.

There is certainly nothing wrong with wanting and having nice things. To do so is God's will for His children. He desires for us to prosper, but He doesn't want us to be greedy. This might be a good time to take a good look at what you are giving and make sure it is a generous amount. I suggest tithing and giving over and beyond the tithe as offerings to missions, the poor, and other good works. Also, I strongly suggest that you help those you know who are in need.

The early church had great power, but they were also constantly involved in meeting one another's needs (Acts 2:43–45). They shared all things in common, so one person's abundance was the answer to another's lack. When you see a need, do you pray about it or do something about it? Once God told me to stop praying for Him to meet needs that I could easily meet myself but simply didn't want to. This is a sobering thought and one we should seriously ponder.

I strongly believe that being a generous giver is one of the best things we can do for ourselves. It prevents us from being self-focused and self-centered, and it causes others to praise God for the provision He has provided through the generous person. Generosity and joy go together. Where you see one, you will see the other.

PROVERBS 22

Proverbs 22:1 teaches us the importance of having a good name and says that it is more desirable than silver or gold. A person's name represents a person's character, so to have a good name means that when people hear your name, they equate it with your good character. When you hear someone's name, you immediately think either positive or negative thoughts about that person, right? Solomon urges us to have a good name, and in order to do that, we must be people of honor, truth, and honesty. We must be people who keep our word and always do what we say we will do.

In years past, a handshake or a person's word was enough to seal a deal, and there was no need for long, tedious contracts. When people gave their word regarding what they would do, they were serious. Even if honoring their commitments required making personal sacrifices or, in some instances, death, they would not break their word. Their name and what it represented meant a great deal to them. I sincerely wish things were still that way.

Our names also represent the way we treat people. Think about it: How many times has someone gotten a bad name in your mind because you have heard that he or she treated someone badly? It is important to the Lord that we treat all people as He would, and that we deal with them the way we want others to deal with us (Matthew 7:12).

The Lord is the maker of both rich and poor, and He does not show partiality (v. 2; Romans 2:11). He is just and fair to everyone regardless of a person's station in life. People may treat a rich person better than a poor one, but that is definitely not God's will. As a matter of fact, He encourages us to show honor to the poor among us (James 2:1–6). As I said, how we treat people is very important to the Lord. If we mistreat them, we will pay the penalty for doing so. "Whoever sows injustice reaps calamity, and the rod they wield in fury will be broken"

> *Do you treat everyone as Jesus would treat them?*

(v. 8). If we oppress the poor to increase our wealth while giving gifts to the rich, we will "come to poverty" (v. 16).

One of the primary themes of Proverbs is relationships. Good relationships with others come from treating people well. I love the old saying that people may not always remember what you said to them, but they will always remember how you made them feel. Always treat people the way you want to be treated and you will more than likely treat everyone with excellence.

THIRTY SAYINGS OF THE WISE

The header "Thirty Sayings of the Wise" is placed just before Proverbs 22:17 and covers the verses through the end of chapter 24. These are the sayings of the sages, who, as I mentioned earlier, were usually older men of greater-than-average wisdom, who had experienced and learned a lot in life. It is always wise to listen to those who have experienced what we have not.

Six of the sayings of the wise are included in the remainder of chapter 22. I will paraphrase them and trust that you will study them more deeply on your own.

Saying 1

> Pay attention and turn your ear to the sayings of the wise; apply your heart to what I teach, for it is pleasing when you keep them in your heart and have all of them ready on your lips. So that your trust may be in the Lord, I teach you today, even you. Have I not written thirty sayings for you, sayings of counsel and knowledge, teaching you to be honest and to speak the truth, so that you bring back truthful reports to those you serve?
>
> Proverbs 22:17–21

In saying 1, we read the instruction to listen to the wise and apply their teachings to our hearts. Wisdom is available in every area of our lives, and if we seek it we will find it. When we find it, we need to apply it to our lives in practical ways. For us to keep wisdom in our hearts and on our lips is "pleasing," says Proverbs 22:18. Wise men and women teach us so that we may learn to trust in the Lord. Proverbs gives us thirty principles of wisdom to counsel us, to help us grow in knowledge, and to teach us to be honest and speak the truth (vv. 20–21).

Notice that the end of verse 21 says we should speak truthfully so that we "bring back truthful reports to those you serve." This reminds me of the story about the boss who asked me to lie for him. Even though I was concerned I might lose my job if I didn't do so, I did tell him no and eventually received a promotion. I think that part of the reason for the promotion was that he knew I was honest and truthful. No matter who we work for, even if we work for ourselves, we serve someone. Ultimately, we all serve God. As we speak the truth, we will always have honest reports.

Saying 2

> Do not exploit the poor because they are poor and do not crush the needy in court, for the Lord will take up their case and will exact life for life.
>
> Proverbs 22:22–23

God is our vindicator, and He always brings justice to us, which means that He makes wrong things right. If we take advantage of someone or take a person to court to collect a debt when we know they are poor and needy, God will vindicate them, and we will lose what we paid trying to collect from them.

Saying 3

> Do not make friends with a hot-tempered person, do
> not associate with one easily angered, or you may learn
> their ways and get yourself ensnared.
>
> Proverbs 22:24–25

I often tell people they could change their lives for the better
if they would simply change some of their friends. I will point
out again that the people with whom we spend our time are
very important, because they can influence us strongly. We
will become like the people we are around.

Spend time with people you admire and want to be like,
and they will benefit you greatly simply by their presence
and example. Ask yourself if you are spending too much time
with someone who does not benefit your spiritual growth. If
so, make a change.

Saying 4

> Do not be one who shakes hands in pledge or puts up
> security for debts; if you lack the means to pay, your
> very bed will be snatched from under you.
>
> Proverbs 22:26–27

Saying 4 reminds us not to agree to be responsible for someone else's debts if they don't pay them. If you do, you may

end up losing what you have because you had to pay a bill for someone else. It may be difficult to tell someone who wants you to cosign a loan for them that you won't do it, but it is better to follow wisdom than to be sorry later. As I mentioned earlier in this book, to cosign means to agree to pay someone's debt if he or she cannot pay it. Anytime you do this, you are taking a chance on losing money for which you have worked hard.

Saying 5

> Do not move an ancient boundary stone set up by your ancestors.
>
> Proverbs 22:28

Today we have boundary lines that mark our property, so we know just how much property we own. These boundaries are recorded in public offices and are official. In Old Testament times, boundary lines were marked with a simple stone. To move a boundary line on property you had inherited—boundaries established by an ancestor—was the same as theft. Ancient boundary stones in Israel were sacred because all land was considered to be a gift from God. So, to move a boundary stone was not only equal to robbery, it was also an act of disrespect toward God. This saying is another encouragement for us to be honest in everything.

Saying 6

> Do you see someone skilled in their work? They will
> serve before kings; they will not serve before officials
> of low rank.
>
> Proverbs 22:29

People who are skilled in their work will be promoted and
serve in high places, not in low places. You see, a skill is
not something we are merely given; it is something we
develop through use over time.
God gives us abilities, but He
expects us to work with and
strengthen them. As we do, we
will become highly skilled in

> *Do you do your best work
> all the time and endeavor
> to improve your skills?*

them. As Proverbs 12:24 says, "Diligent hands will rule, but
laziness ends in forced labor."

Each of these sayings is given to us by wise men who
learned these principles through experience. As we heed this
good advice, we can save ourselves a great deal of trouble and
position ourselves for happiness and success.

PROVERBS 23

Proverbs 23 covers sayings 7 through 19. Several of them are short, but they are still wise and will educate us in right behavior.

Saying 7

> When you sit to dine with a ruler, note well what is before you, and put a knife to your throat if you are given to gluttony. Do not crave his delicacies, for that food is deceptive.
>
> Proverbs 23:1–3

This saying advises us on how to behave ourselves and what kind of manners to use when we sit down to eat with a person of power or authority. It would apply, however, whenever we sit down to eat, as it teaches us not to be gluttonous (meaning to take or eat too much food). Saying 7 also teaches us that we cannot judge a person's character by what he serves to eat at a dinner or by anything that he owns. We need to be careful not to be impressed with people's titles or possessions without truly knowing what kind of person they are. "Delicacies" may be "deceptive" (v. 3).

Saying 8

> Do not wear yourself out to get rich; do not trust your
> own cleverness. Cast but a glance at riches, and they
> are gone, for they will surely sprout wings and fly off to
> the sky like an eagle.
>
> Proverbs 23:4–5

Riches can be very deceitful, and you should not exhaust
yourself trying to attain them (v. 4). Riches can be gone in an
instant, so make sure you live for what has true and lasting
value. Many people spend excessive amounts of time trying
to make more and more money while ignoring things that are
truly important. Some never realize the mistakes they have
made, but many do realize them, only to find out it is too
late to correct their misspent time. Always put God first, family next, and then work. If you work so much you have no
time for God, family, or friends, then you are working too
much and need to make a change.

Saying 9

> Do not eat the food of a begrudging host, do not crave
> his delicacies; for he is the kind of person who is always
> thinking about the cost. "Eat and drink," he says to
> you, but his heart is not with you. You will vomit up
> the little you have eaten and will have wasted your
> compliments.
>
> Proverbs 23:6–8

I have taught and written often on Proverbs 23:7, which says in some translations that as a person "thinks in his heart, so is he" (NKJV, KJV). This means that we become what we think about and indicates that our thoughts have much more power over our lives than we may realize.

The NIV translation renders this verse differently, indicating that a person can appear to be one way, yet in his heart be entirely different. For example, someone may invite you to a feast while hoping you don't eat much, because he is thinking about how much the meal will cost him. He is a begrudging host. He says, "Eat all you want! Drink all you want!" But in his heart, he does not really want you to take too much of his food or drink. This teaches us that it is important for us to be genuine with our words. We should not speak in ways we think will impress the hearer when our words do not represent our true feelings. Our inner life (the hidden person of the heart) reveals who we really are.

Saying 10

Do not speak to fools, for they will scorn your prudent words.

Proverbs 23:9

When speaking to a foolish person, our words will be wasted because he or she either doesn't want to listen or will consider the words contemptible and worthless. Foolish people are usually not interested in learning from anyone else. This is, in fact, why they are foolish.

Saying 11

> Do not move an ancient boundary stone or encroach
> on the fields of the fatherless, for their Defender is
> strong; he will take up their case against you.
>
> Proverbs 23:10–11

This saying warns us again not to change boundary lines or
attempt to steal land from the fatherless (v. 10). It also notes
that God is their strong defender and "will take up their case
against" anyone who tries to treat them dishonestly (v. 11). I
explained the seriousness of moving boundary stones in my
comments on saying 5, so I want to focus here on the fatherless. God seems to be especially fond of those who are fatherless, and we are instructed to help and care for them, not to
take advantage of them. It is comforting to know that God
defends those who cannot defend themselves.

Saying 12

> Apply your heart to instruction and your ears to words
> of knowledge.
>
> Proverbs 23:12

The word *apply* means to put to practical use, so the writer
is telling us not only to hear words of knowledge but to use
them in our everyday lives. Wisdom is said to be the correct use of knowledge. Simply knowing something does

not benefit us if we don't apply it to our lives. Many people are proud of what they know, but more importantly, is God proud of their actions? Glorifying Him with our behavior is much better than having knowledge we never apply.

Saying 13

> Do not withhold discipline from a child; if you punish them with the rod, they will not die. Punish them with the rod and save them from death.
>
> Proverbs 23:13–14

This saying deals with correcting and disciplining children. Punishing them "with the rod" refers to spanking. Spanking children as a means of punishment was popular in the past, but most people today prefer to discipline in other ways. Many people have had parents who beat them, and that is definitely not God's will.

Some people may take this scripture out of context. Shepherds used their rods to lead and manage their flock, and to defend them against wild animals. Bible Study Tools says that the shepherd's rod is "figurative of divine guidance or care."

This reference to the rod in saying 13 indicates that using it pertains more to teaching children right from wrong than hitting them with a stick or anything else. Children need discipline, but it should be given in love, not in anger. God "disciplines those he loves" (Proverbs 3:12).

Saying 14

My son, if your heart is wise, then my heart will be glad indeed; my inmost being will rejoice when your lips speak what is right.

Proverbs 23:15–16

If we apply saying 14 spiritually, we can see that when we are wise, it makes God's heart glad, and He rejoices when we "speak what is right" (v. 16). This calls to our attention again the thread running throughout Proverbs that reminds us repeatedly of the importance of using wisdom in our thoughts and speech. Throughout God's Word we can find encouragement to think and speak wisely, and I pray we will all see how important these areas are. In the *Battlefield of the Mind Bible*, you can find an index to many verses pertaining to thoughts and words, and you can see those verses highlighted within the text of the Bible itself.

Saying 15

Do not let your heart envy sinners, but always be zealous for the fear of the Lord. There is surely a future hope for you, and your hope will not be cut off.

Proverbs 23:17–18

Many believers can be tempted to be jealous of sinners at times, but we should resist that temptation and cultivate a vibrant fear of the Lord instead. The ungodly may have material things that we don't have or do things that God's Word does not allow us to do, but we live for eternity, not momentary pleasure. As believers, God wants us to enjoy our lives, and we can do that without entering into sinful entertainment.

True believers in Christ can look forward to a future hope that is sure and will never "be cut off" (v. 18). Thinking about spending eternity with God in a place that is beautiful beyond anything we can imagine—where there is no sorrow, no death, no crying, no misery

> *Do you look forward to eternity?*

of any kind, no pain, no sickness, and joy unspeakable— helps us not to envy anything an unbeliever has.

Saying 16

> Listen, my son, and be wise, and set your heart on the right path: Do not join those who drink too much wine or gorge themselves on meat, for drunkards and gluttons become poor, and drowsiness clothes them in rags.
>
> Proverbs 23:19–21

This saying encourages us to live disciplined lives, to be wise and set our hearts, meaning our minds, "on the right path" (v. 19). It goes on to say warn against those who eat and drink too much, asserting that those who do so will become poor and lazy.

God has given us many good things to enjoy. Food and drink are two of those things, but we are to consume them in moderation. We are free to enjoy all that God has created, but too much of a good thing becomes a bad thing.

I hope you are as amazed as I am by how practical the Proverbs are. I see it more and more as we go through them. They are giving us practical, easy-to-understand advice on how to enjoy life without allowing ourselves to be controlled by anything it offers.

Saying 17

> Listen to your father, who gave you life, and do not despise your mother when she is old. Buy the truth and do not sell it—wisdom, instruction and insight as well. The father of a righteous child has great joy; a man who fathers a wise son rejoices in him. May your father and mother rejoice; may she who gave you birth be joyful!
>
> Proverbs 23:22–25

Not everyone has had positive experiences with their parents. Among those who have had good parents, not all are willing to listen to their fathers. This is a serious mistake. They could avoid a lot of trouble if they would be humble enough to listen to good advice when a father offers it.

When verse 22 encourages us to honor our mothers when they are old, I think it refers not only to the way we feel about our parents as they age but also to how we treat them. Let me encourage you to always show honor to your parents and give them any loving care they need, even if they were not particularly kind to you as you grew up.

God wants parents to be able to rejoice in their children (vv. 24–25), and that can only happen when we live righteous lives and apply wisdom, instruction, and insight to our lives.

Saying 18

> My son, give me your heart and let your eyes delight in my ways, for an adulterous woman is a deep pit, and a wayward wife is a narrow well. Like a bandit she lies in wait and multiplies the unfaithful among men.
>
> Proverbs 23:26–28

This saying includes another warning about the adulterous woman. Sexual infidelity is at an all-time high. According to the American Association for Marriage and Family Therapy, roughly 20 percent of spouses are unfaithful to their marriage partner. Because of the thousands upon thousands of sexual images placed in front of us today through media and advertising, temptation is also at an all-time high. Most people watch television, and a Kaiser Family Foundation study found that two out of every three shows (excluding news, sports, and children's shows) in their study sample included sexual content. Be wise and don't look at things that will tempt you to be unfaithful. God's Word teaches us to guard our ways (Psalm 39:1; 1 Timothy 6:20), and today especially, we need to be vigilant to do so.

Saying 19

> Who has woe? Who has sorrow? Who has strife? Who
> has complaints? Who has needless bruises? Who has
> bloodshot eyes? Those who linger over wine, who go
> to sample bowls of mixed wine. Do not gaze at wine
> when it is red, when it sparkles in the cup, when it goes
> down smoothly! In the end it bites like a snake and
> poisons like a viper. Your eyes will see strange sights,
> and your mind will imagine confusing things. You will
> be like one sleeping on the high seas, lying on top of
> the rigging. "They hit me," you will say, "but I'm not
> hurt! They beat me, but I don't feel it! When will I
> wake up so I can find another drink?"
>
> Proverbs 23:29–35

Saying 19 covers the final seven verses in Proverbs 23—all
warnings to those who linger too long over wine (v. 30). In
other words, it is written to those who drink too much wine
or are tempted to do so. That person will have sorrow, strife,
complaints, needless bruises, and bloodshot eyes (v. 29).

Wine "sparkles in the cup" and looks inviting (v. 31). "It
goes down smoothly," but eventually "it bites like a snake"
(vv. 31–32). It can cause us to lose touch with reality and
cause our minds to become confused (v. 33). People who
drink too much also get a sense of disconnection from their
bodies and their minds, causing them to lose physical aware-
ness and good judgment. Excessive drinking can also cause

people to think when they first wake up in the morning, *Where can I "find another drink"?* (v. 35).

This sounds like a sad and useless way to live, so please remember: If you drink alcohol, please do it in moderation, and never let it become something you must have in order to be happy and satisfied.

PROVERBS 24

This chapter contains the final eleven sayings, plus some additional advice from the wise.

Saying 20

> Do not envy the wicked, do not desire their company;
> for their hearts plot violence, and their lips talk about
> making trouble.
>
> Proverbs 24:1–2

As I have mentioned before, there are times when the wicked seem to prosper more than the righteous. Sometimes that causes the righteous to feel tempted to be jealous of them, but God always brings justice in the end. True prosperity goes far beyond possessions or wealth; it includes good relationships with God and with other people, peace, and joy. The wicked (ungodly) may have possessions, but they don't have the things that are truly valuable.

Some people, even Christians, like to be with people who appear to be important because of what they own or the positions they hold. We are much better off spending time with people who have a godly character than with those who choose not to live according to God's Word.

Saying 20 goes on to assert that in their hearts the wicked plot violence and that "their lips talk about making trouble" (v. 2). They frequently gain their possessions and wealth through dishonest means and look for every opportunity to gain more for themselves with no concern for who they hurt or take advantage of in order to do so.

Saying 21

> By wisdom a house is built, and through understanding it is established; through knowledge its rooms are filled with rare and beautiful treasures.
>
> Proverbs 24:3–4

We see three of the seven foundational principles of the Book of Proverbs in this one saying: wisdom, understanding, and knowledge.

Building a home in which a family can reside peacefully is very important. We spend much of our time at home, and our homes should be comfortable places that we enjoy. The atmosphere in our homes should be peaceful, loving, and God-honoring. Applying the principles in Proverbs will ensure that will happen.

Are you doing all you can do to make sure your home is peaceful?

In order to maintain peace in your home, you will need

to slow down and think about your decisions, because if you rush through life, you will certainly miss wisdom. Don't allow yourself to get upset about things you cannot do anything about. Pray, cast your anxiety on God (1 Peter 5:7), and hold on to your peace. As you continue to trust God, He will solve your problems.

Saying 22

The wise prevail through great power, and those who have knowledge muster their strength. Surely you need guidance to wage war, and victory is won through many advisers.

Proverbs 24:5–6

The wise have great power that enables them to prevail in difficult circumstances (v. 5). And those who have knowledge also have strength and are able to call upon it when they need it (v. 5). Life can present us with many difficulties, and during hard times we need spiritual power and strength to help us make it through them to victory.

We are in a spiritual war against evil, and we need to seek advice from the wise to wage that war successfully. We gain victory through many good advisers (v. 6), but we need to be sure they are godly advisers. Psalm 1:1 says we are not to take advice from the ungodly. When you ask for advice, be sure you know the character of the person from whom you request it.

Saying 23

> Wisdom is too high for fools; in the assembly at the gate they must not open their mouths.
>
> Proverbs 24:7

Fools (morally deficient people) cannot grasp or understand wisdom, because it is "too high" for them (v. 7). The best thing foolish people can do is not open their mouths. However, most fools are too foolish to know they are fools, so they continue bringing trouble into their lives. They often spend their lives blaming others and never have enough courage to be honest about themselves.

Let me encourage you to be bold enough to compare your behavior with the instructions in Proverbs. When you realize you have not been living wisely, ask God to forgive you for wrongdoing and help you learn all about wisdom and apply it to your life.

Saying 24

> Whoever plots evil will be known as a schemer. The schemes of folly are sin, and people detest a mocker.
>
> Proverbs 24:8–9

Schemers are involved in making secret, underhanded plans that will help them get what they want. They are selfish and view everything in terms of how it might help them.

The mocker makes fun of or derides things they should respect—such as God and His Word, or other holy things that the fear of the Lord would prevent a person from ridiculing. We should have the utmost respect for holy things and never make light of them. Being disrespectful to God or His people is one of the most foolish things a person can do. The Bible mentions mockers frequently and never in a positive way. They cause a great deal of trouble for themselves and for those who listen to them.

Saying 25

> If you falter in a time of trouble, how small is your strength! Rescue those being led away to death; hold back those staggering toward slaughter. If you say, "But we knew nothing about this," does not he who weighs the heart perceive it? Does not he who guards your life know it? Will he not repay everyone according to what they have done?
>
> Proverbs 24:10–12

If we falter or give up "in a time of trouble," then we do not have much strength (v. 10). Our spiritual strength and character are tested in difficult times, not in good ones. It is important to remain constant and content in good times and bad.

Proverbs 24:11 encourages us to help those headed for trouble and to try to get them to repent and move in a positive direction before it is too late. God knows our hearts, and not only should we be obedient ourselves, but we should also help those who are "staggering toward slaughter" (v. 11) or being led away to death. When we see people living unwisely, we can easily think, *That is none of my business*, but according to this wise saying, we have a responsibility to try to turn sinners to righteousness whenever possible.

God repays us according to our actions (v. 12), and trying to help others is always a good thing to do.

Saying 26

> Eat honey, my son, for it is good; honey from the comb is sweet to your taste. Know also that wisdom is like honey for you: If you find it, there is a future hope for you, and your hope will not be cut off.
>
> Proverbs 24:13–14

This wise saying compares sweet honey to wisdom (v. 14). Like honey to our mouths, wisdom will make our lives sweet and good if we heed it. When we find wisdom, it gives us hope for the future, and that hope will never "be cut off" (v. 14). It will never fail or disappoint us.

Hope is vitally important, because it keeps us from being discouraged and depressed over current circumstances. While writing this book, I had a tooth implant finalized. About a week later, it was still hurting. By that time, I was out of town and could not get to the dentist for another week. However, I spoke to my dentist by phone, and he assured me that he would be able to take the tooth off the post and file it down so it would not apply pressure to my other teeth. After speaking with him, I felt better mentally and emotionally because I had hope for a solution.

"Hope deferred makes the heart sick" (Proverbs 13:12). We need hope, and those who walk in wisdom will always have it.

Saying 27

> Do not lurk like a thief near the house of the righteous, do not plunder their dwelling place; for though the righteous fall seven times, they rise again, but the wicked stumble when calamity strikes.
>
> Proverbs 24:15–16

Proverbs 24:15 warns the wicked not to plot evil against "the righteous." Believers are the righteous (2 Corinthians 5:21), and God is our protector. To steal from the righteous or to harm them in other ways is not wise. The righteous person can fall down seven times and "rise again" each time (v. 16). It is difficult to defeat the righteous because God is on their side.

The wicked, however, always stumble and fall when difficulty comes their way (v. 16). They are weak and have no inner resources to help them remain strong in times of trouble. They can only be happy and peaceful when all their circumstances are pleasant.

Saying 28

> Do not gloat when your enemy falls; when they stumble, do not let your heart rejoice, or the Lord will see and disapprove and turn his wrath away from them.
>
> Proverbs 24:17–18

This saying is one that I love, and it is an important one to hide in our hearts. It says that we should not be happy when bad things happen to our enemies. The Lord disapproves of this, and in fact, it makes Him angry.

It is so easy and natural to be happy when someone who has hurt or taken advantage of us must face the consequences of their actions. Our first thought is usually, *Good. You deserve it.* But that is not the attitude God wants us to have. He is our Father, and He wants us to imitate Him in every situation (1 Peter 2:21). Being able to pray for our enemies, bless them, and have true compassion on them when they encounter trouble is powerful (Matthew 5:44). This ability is not based on our feelings; we can only do it with the help of the Holy Spirit and by making decisions according to God's Word.

Do you feel compassion toward those who have hurt you and believe the best about them?

Remember, Jesus prayed for those who crucified Him, saying, "Father, forgive them, for they do not know what they are doing" (Luke 23:34). And when Stephen was being stoned to death, he prayed, "Lord, do not hold this sin against them" (Acts 7:60). When people hurt us, we tend to assume they have done it on purpose. But we must remember that "hurting people hurt people" and often are not even aware of their actions. This does not mean they are not responsible for what they do, but that we should trust God to deal with them in His way and in His timing and never be happy when they fall or face difficulty.

Saying 29

> Do not fret because of evildoers or be envious of the wicked, for the evildoer has no future hope, and the lamp of the wicked will be snuffed out.
>
> Proverbs 24:19–20

This saying reminds us again not to "fret because of evildoers or be envious of the wicked" (v. 19). Verse 20 adds, "The evildoer has no future hope." Evildoers may have possessions, but they have no hope! Eventually "the lamp of the wicked will be snuffed out" unless they change (v. 20). To help us understand this idea, the Good News Bible renders this verse to say that the wicked will have "nothing to look forward to." Just imagine living with nothing to look forward to. It certainly doesn't sound very inviting.

Psalm 37 is a wonderful psalm about the attitude we should have toward the wicked. I read it often because it gives me grace to live in a wicked world, knowing that in the end "the righteous will inherit the land and dwell in it forever" (Psalm 37:29). This psalm tells us not to fret over

the evildoer, because he will soon "wither" and "die away" (v.
2), but if we "take delight in the Lord" and find our joy and
peace in Him, He will give us the desires of our hearts (v. 4).
There is no reason for us to envy the ungodly, because God
will always take care of us and give us what is best for us at
the right time. I cannot emphasize it enough: Trust in the
Lord at all times!

I suppose the matter of a believer's attitude toward the
ungodly is repeated often in Proverbs because Satan tempts
us to resent the fact that those who do evil may often seem to
prosper more than those who do what is right, and at times
those who do right appear to be worse off than the ungodly.
But for those who remain steadfast in the Lord, reward will
come.

Saying 30

Fear the Lord and the king, my son, and do not join
with rebellious officials, for those two will send sudden
destruction on them, and who knows what calamities
they can bring?

Proverbs 24:21–22

The thirty sayings of the wise end with an encouragement to
fear the Lord and not to join with the rebellious because "sudden destruction" will come upon them (vv. 21–22). We are
not to rejoice in this, but it is a fact nonetheless. It is impossible to continue doing evil and never reap the harvest of the

seed that has been sown, just as it is impossible to continue doing right and never reap the harvest of good seed sown.

Every time we make a good decision and walk in wisdom instead of foolishness, we should look forward to our reward. We should never try to do what is right simply to gain a reward. We need to do right because it pleases God, but we can also know with certainty that blessings are the by-products of wise, godly living.

MORE SAYINGS OF THE WISE

Proverbs 24 includes eleven additional verses that are also sayings of the wise, though the text does not note them as such.

These also are sayings of the wise: To show partiality in judging is not good: Whoever says to the guilty, "You are innocent," will be cursed by peoples and denounced by nations. But it will go well with those who convict the guilty, and rich blessing will come on them. An honest answer is like a kiss on the lips. Put your outdoor work in order and get your fields ready; after that, build your house. Do not testify against your neighbor without cause—would you use your lips to mislead? Do not say, "I'll do to them as they have done to me; I'll pay them back for what they did." I went past the field of a sluggard, past the vineyard of someone who has no sense; thorns had come up everywhere, the ground was covered with weeds, and the stone wall was in ruins. I applied my heart to what I observed and learned a lesson from what I saw: A little sleep, a little slumber, a little folding of the hands to rest—and poverty will come on you like a thief and scarcity like an armed man.

Proverbs 24:23–34

We are reminded not to "show partiality in judging" (v. 23) and not to tell the guilty they are innocent when we know they are not, because that brings curses (v. 24). But those who convict the guilty will be richly blessed (v. 25). We need to be courageous enough to stand up to evil and deal with it in a godly way.

Sometimes doing the right thing is difficult if doing it causes us to struggle. We may have compassion on people who have gotten themselves in trouble, but sparing them the consequences of their actions may be inviting them to do the same things again. We may have a personal relationship with the one who has done wrong and let that tempt us to make excuses for their wrong behavior instead of dealing with them without partiality. Obeying God often requires us to live beyond our emotions and do what we know is right, no matter how we feel.

Proverbs 24:26 tells us, "An honest answer is like a kiss on the lips." We should never say, "I'll do to them as they have done to me! I'll pay them back for what they did." God is our vindicator, and He will reward us if we trust Him, wait on Him, and don't take matters into our own hands (Proverbs 20:22; Romans 12:19).

Chapter 24 ends by reminding us that everything the sluggard has will come to ruin because he won't lift a finger to take care of any of it (vv. 30–34). We can learn a lesson from watching the lives of lazy people. They have the same opportunities to prosper that others have, but they never flourish because they are unwilling to work or make an effort. We can learn much wisdom from the Proverbs and from life's experiences. To be wise is surely the best choice anyone can make.

PROVERBS 25

Proverbs 25 opens with these words: "These are more proverbs of Solomon, compiled by the men of Hezekiah king of Judah:" (v. 1).

SEEK AND YOU WILL FIND

According to Proverbs 25:2, "It is the glory of God to conceal a matter," and "to search out a matter is the glory of kings." When God hides something from us, it is honorable and excellent (glorious) because it causes us to seek and search for answers. For this reason, let me encourage you to always be willing to dig deep for the gold that is found in God's Word. If you don't understand something you read in the Bible, seek God for answers. He says that if you seek and keep on seeking, "you will find" (Matthew 7:7).

Much of the joy we find in discovering the answers we need or in learning something new is in seeking. It is an excellent (glorious) thing for leaders (kings) and for people in general to put some effort into finding the answers to what God has concealed. This is one reason I strongly suggest that you *study* God's Word rather than simply read it.

We can find many treasures in Scripture by seeking, but there are also things hidden in the heart of God that human beings cannot discover, no matter how diligently we search. This means there are times when we must be at peace with not knowing something. God's ways are higher than our ways (Isaiah 55:9), and His judgments are "unsearchable" and "His ways past finding out!" (Romans 11:33 NKJV). This doesn't mean that we can never find what we need to know, but sometimes, certain things in God's heart would not be good for us to know. If we knew everything about everything, we would have no need to trust God. Trusting Him is something He wants us to do at all times.

Walking with God requires trust and patience—trusting God when we don't understand and being willing to wait for His timing in our lives. Allowing us to go through such tests is one way He removes the impurities from our hearts so we can eventually serve Him wholeheartedly rather than half-heartedly. Just as dross must be removed from silver before it can be used to make a vessel (v. 4), so our impurities need to be removed in order for God to use us fully as He desires.

WAIT PATIENTLY FOR PROMOTION

Proverbs 25:6–7 teaches us to wait to be called forward instead of advancing ourselves. Waiting for someone in authority to invite us to come up is much better than being humiliated by putting ourselves forth and being asked to move back.

I remember a man who accepted a job to work for us.

Within a few days, he began making all kinds of suggestions about changes we could implement to make things better. He wrote me letters and asked for appointments to talk with me about his ideas. When his ideas were not accepted, he became adamant and pushy about them. It was obvious he had a proud and haughty attitude, and he was not walking in wisdom at all.

We barely knew this man, and it was not his place to tell me how to run the ministry. That doesn't mean that I don't take advice from people, but when I do, it comes from time-honored and trusted friends or peers, not someone I met a few days ago. Eventually the man had to be let go, and chances are that he repeated the same behavior in other organizations until he hopefully saw the error of his ways.

I've seen people join churches and immediately want to be put in charge of something. They spare no words in telling the leaders how talented and capable they are. This is an inappropriate approach. It would be better for them to pray and wait for God to bring attention to them, rather than trying to call it to themselves.

A TRUSTWORTHY FRIEND

"Like a snow-cooled drink at harvest time is a trustworthy messenger to the one who sends him; he refreshes the spirit of his master" (v. 13). Trusted friends and co-workers are extremely valuable. Sadly, many people today can't be trusted to be discreet and, as you may remember, discretion is one of the foundational principles of the Book of Proverbs. When you can trust people to do something exactly as you ask them to do it, when you ask them to do it, you have a precious gift. I have a few people like that in my life, and I value them highly. Being able to depend on a person is definitely refreshing.

Let's make sure we are trustworthy and then trust God to bring other trustworthy people into our lives. Proverbs 25:19 says that reliance on an unfaithful person in a time of trouble is "like a broken tooth or a lame foot." We know, or can imagine, how a broken tooth would hurt. Having an unfaithful friend is like that—exceedingly painful. The pain is emotional rather than physical, but it is miserable nonetheless. We may as well do a job ourselves if we cannot trust the one to whom we delegate the work to do it properly.

I love working with people I don't have to check on to make sure they are doing what they should be doing. God is trustworthy and faithful, and we should strive to be the same way. One comment the Bible makes about Moses, a man God used greatly, was that he was faithful (Hebrews 3:5). If we want God to be able to use us, then He must be able to trust us. He often starts by giving us something small over which to be faithful. If we pass that test, then He gives us more (Matthew 25:23).

> *Do you consider yourself to be a trustworthy and faithful person?*

Zechariah 4:10 says not to despise the day of small beginnings (AMP). This means not to think any job is too small or any assignment is too insignificant for you. Put your whole heart into whatever God gives you to do, and as you are faithful in the little things, you will be put "in charge of many things" (Matthew 25:23).

TAKING A NEIGHBOR TO COURT

Today, anyone can file a lawsuit and sue another person, and doing so is considered to be a basic right. But God encouraged the New Testament believers to settle things between themselves rather than taking their matters into a worldly court system (1 Corinthians 6:1). Proverbs mentions taking a neighbor to court several times and tells us never to bear false witness against a neighbor or to ruin their reputation. Proverbs 25:8 says not to be hasty in going to court because your neighbor might put you to shame in the end. Once again, we read that wisdom waits and is never hasty.

Anger can motivate us to take quick action that we will regret later. It is always best to sleep on a decision like this and think it over for a day or two before taking action. Court proceedings are lengthy and expensive, and the time you put into settling something in this manner may not be worth what you get out of it.

There are times when a lawsuit may be necessary if you have truly been wronged and have no other recourse, but legal recourse is not something to take hastily.

HOW TO TREAT YOUR ENEMIES

"If your enemy is hungry, give him food to eat; if he is thirsty, give him water to drink. In doing this, you will heap burning coals on his head, and the Lord will reward you" (vv. 21–22).

We may initially think "burning coals" refers to something that would harm our enemies, but they are quite the opposite. They represent the love we show to our enemies. If we love our enemies, God rewards us (Luke 6:35). Loving people who hurt, offend, or otherwise mistreat us is not easy to do, but it is actually easier than being filled with bitterness and hatred. Consistently expressing love to our enemies can melt their hard hearts and lead them to turn to God in repentance.

Proverbs 25:21–22 teaches us to help our enemies in practical ways. When people have done us wrong and we help them in love, they usually do not understand it. But love speaks more loudly to them than anything else, and they are compelled to pay attention to it.

Are you angry with anyone right now? If so, are you willing to forgive them completely and help them if and when they need help?

The way to have fewer enemies is to always believe the best of everyone. Paul encouraged the Corinthians to do this when he wrote that love always believes the best of everyone, and it never fails (1 Corinthians 13:4–8). Loving people is much more enjoyable than hating them, even if they don't deserve our love. After all, we don't deserve God's love, but He gives it to us unconditionally and without interruption. He may not love everything we do, but He always loves us. Can we be the same way with others?

GOOD NEWS

"Like cold water to a weary soul is good news from a distant land" (v. 25). I love good news, and I am sure you do, too. The world seems filled with bad news, so any good news we get is very refreshing. I pray for God to send me good news quite often.

Let me suggest that when you do know something positive, you spread it around. Sometimes we are quicker to spread bad news than to share good news. I have heard that there is a saying in the media industry: "Good news is no news." They want negative or sensational stories that will catch people's attention, but I usually don't even bother reading such reports. Reading or listening to too many negative things actually makes me tired.

God calls us to edify and encourage one another and stir up one another to good works (Hebrews 10:24). He does not want us to tear down and discourage one another by spreading bad reports. When you know something positive or uplifting, call someone and share it. Hearing good news will be like cold water to a weary soul.

SELF-CONTROL

Proverbs 25 ends with an exhortation to use self-control. If we don't, then Solomon says we are like a city whose walls are broken down (v. 28). In other words, we leave a place for our enemy, Satan, to enter our lives and wreak havoc. We are to give him no place, which means not to allow him an opportunity to influence us. Some people say, "I just don't have any self-control," or "I am just not disciplined." But that is not true because God has given us both self-control and self-discipline (2 Timothy 1:7 AMP, NIV). We may not be using them, but we have the power to do so. Becoming self-disciplined is like developing muscles. Everyone has muscles, but they may be tiny through lack of use. As we begin to use them, they will grow.

Solomon says, "It is not good to eat too much honey," nor is it good to "search out matters that are too deep" for us (v. 27). Both of these situations require self-control. In Solomon's day, honey was probably the sweetest taste available. He has compared it to wisdom because, like wisdom, it offers many benefits. He even encourages eating honey in Proverbs 24:13. Even though honey is sweet and good, here, he notes that *too much* honey definitely is "not good." In fact, it would ultimately make a person sick. Today we have way too many options, and many people are overweight and unhealthy because they do not use self-control concerning sugary foods. It looks like Solomon's wisdom was right after all!

Not searching out things that are too deep for us also

helps us have peace in our lives. I am referring to the torment of continual reasoning in which we try to figure out and understand issues or situations for which we have no answers. I don't think it is wrong to ponder things before God. In fact, I believe He encourages us to do so. But when we think so much that we become confused, it is time to drop the matter and simply say, "I ask You to reveal this to me, Lord, if You want me to know it. Until then I will trust You."

Too much of anything can become a problem. Solomon writes in Ecclesiastes 3:1, "There is a time for everything," and that all things should be done at the right time. We are wise to use moderation in all things, meaning to allow ourselves just enough but not too much of anything. This helps us live balanced lives and keeps the doors of our lives closed to the enemy.

PROVERBS 26

Proverbs 26 covers only three subjects: the fool, the lazy person, and the proper and improper use of words. We have already examined these topics, but since the Holy Spirit thought they were important to mention again, I will comment on all three.

THE FOOL

The first twelve verses of Proverbs 26 deal with foolishness. Verses 1 and 3 say that "honor is not fitting for a fool" but he deserves a rod for his back. In other words, acclaim is not appropriate for someone who acts foolishly. Instead, that person deserves a rod, meaning correction, in order to behave properly. Verse 4 says, "Do not answer a fool according to his folly, or you yourself will be just like him." Then verse 5 notes that, on the other hand, not answering a fool will cause him to think he is wise. We must be discerning about when and how to respond when people act foolishly. Jesus sometimes answered people who asked foolish questions; at other times He was silent. We can trust God to give us wisdom in this area and show us what to say or not say.

"Sending a message by the hands of a fool is like cutting off one's feet or drinking poison" (v. 6). This sounds serious, doesn't it? In verse 7, we read that a proverb (saying of wisdom) in the mouth of a fool is useless, like a lame leg or like a thornbush in the hand of a drunkard (v. 9). Proverbs 26:10 says that hiring a fool is "like an archer who wounds at random" (v. 10). In only ten verses thus far, we can see that nothing good comes from dealing with foolish people.

Verse 11 offers a graphic picture of how fools behave: "As a dog returns to its vomit, so fools repeat their folly." Another way to phrase this is to say that fools never learn. They continue to do foolish things. Even when those actions or behaviors have done no good or have brought harm to themselves or to others, they repeat them.

There is "more hope for a fool" than for a person who is "wise in their own eyes" (v. 12). The Amplified Bible, Classic Edition refers to the fool in this verse as "self-confident." God wants us to be confident *in Him*, but His Word never encourages us to be confident in ourselves. We hear a lot about self-confidence in the secular world and can go to endless conferences and find exhaustive resources regarding the subject. But God tells us to find our self-confidence in *His* confidence. I like to say that I am an "everything nothing." I am everything in Christ and can do all things through Him (Philippians 4:13), but in and of myself I am nothing. No good thing dwells in my flesh (Romans 7:18), and apart from Him I can do nothing (John 15:5).

Always remember to lean and rely on God in everything

you do, even in things you have done successfully thousands of times. Reliance on Him honors and pleases Him.

I wrote my own definition of a fool and included it in chapter 1, but I want to repeat it here: A fool is morally deficient, hasty in making decisions, and too quick to speak without thinking. He is probably not prudent with finances and makes poor decisions in all areas of life. He thinks more highly of himself than he should. He is probably lazy and does not exercise self-control. He has an attitude of entitlement, thinking he should be given what he has not worked for or earned. I am sure he lacks appreciation and is ungrateful. He most likely murmurs and complains regularly. He gossips, falls in with bad company, and has no reverential fear and awe of God.

Let us pray daily that we will not behave foolishly, but instead walk in the wisdom God has given us.

THE LAZY PERSON

Have you ever noticed that some people can look right at something that obviously needs to be done and simply ignore it? This describes a lazy person, and Proverbs 26:13–16 teaches us much about those who are lazy.

People who are lazy see a problem but do nothing about it (vv. 13–15). According to verse 16, lazy people believe themselves to be wiser "than seven people who answer discreetly." Lazy people are quick to blame others for whatever they lack, and they make excuses for everything they do wrong. They live according to their feelings, not the Word of God. People who are lazy will end up with nothing while being jealous of others. They will be filled with self-pity, thinking that life is not fair to them, while ignoring their own responsibilities.

Being a hard worker is a godly trait. Of course, we need to rest, and God establishes that in His Word (Matthew 11:28–29; Hebrews 4:9), but hard work is good for the soul. We are created for accomplishment and to use the gifts God has given us to help build His kingdom. A person does not need to have pulpit ministry to be "in ministry." We are all in ministry if we choose to serve and glorify God in whatever we do. It is not important that we do what the world would call great, but that we do what God asks us to do, no matter how great or small it may be. Sometimes being faithful to something small is more difficult than being faithful to something large. Let me encourage you: Bloom where you are planted, and know that even if you are hidden from people, God sees you and is preparing your reward.

> *Are you active and diligent, always doing what needs to be done?*

THE PROPER AND IMPROPER USE OF WORDS

Proverbs 26:17–28 teaches us how to use our words properly and warns us of what can happen if we use them improperly. Verses 17–19 teach us that those who rush into quarrels or arguments that are none of their business are like those who grab "a stray dog by the ears" (v. 17). They run the risk of being bitten and harmed. People who deceive their neighbors and then say, "I was only joking!" (v. 19) are like maniacs "shooting flaming arrows of death" (v. 18).

According to verse 20, gossip cannot continue if we stop spreading it, just as a fire cannot keep burning if we stop adding wood to it. People who are quarrelsome keep strife going; they are like someone who keeps putting charcoal on a fire (v. 21), causing it to keep burning, getting hotter and hotter.

"The words of a gossip are like choice morsels; they go down to the inmost parts" of those to whom we spread rumors (v. 22). We should realize that when we gossip and spread rumors about someone, the person to whom we gossip may develop a negative opinion of the one we're talking about. When someone tells us something unkind or negative about another person, even if we don't want to believe what we have heard, it still tends to make us view the person more suspiciously than we did before we heard the rumor. Spreading gossip is like feeding people little pieces of poison; it poisons their attitudes or opinions about the one being gossiped about.

"Enemies disguise themselves with their lips" (v. 24). They say things to make themselves look good, "but in their hearts they harbor deceit. Though their speech is charming, do not believe them" (vv. 24–25). We have all encountered people whose speech is charming. Many times, smooth speech serves to cover up bad intentions, so we need to ask the Holy Spirit to help us discern when people are speaking truthfully, with purity of heart, and when they are using elo-quence to disguise bad motives.

Proverbs 26:27 says that whoever digs a pit for someone else will fall into it. Verse 27 also says that if one person rolls a stone onto someone else, the stone will roll back on the person pushing it. This is another way of reminding us that we reap what we sow. If we want others to do good things for us, then we must do good things for others.

"A lying tongue hates those it hurts, and a flattering mouth works ruin" (v. 28). To flatter someone is to offer insincere compliments. We can easily be deceived by such flattery because we all appreciate and enjoy compliments. But we should be discerning and endeavor to know which compliments are genuine and which ones are deceitful and motivated by greed or impure desire.

PROVERBS 27

Solomon begins Proverbs 27 by telling us not to boast about tomorrow because we don't know what each day may hold (v. 1). To boast means to talk with excessive pride about our accomplishments, possessions, or achievements. It means to brag, gloat, or show off. While boasting is expressed through our words, I think it primarily comes from an arrogant attitude or condition of the heart. We should form the habit of humbly submitting all of our plans to God and realize we cannot do anything tomorrow unless He gives it to us. One saying I like is, "If you show off, don't be surprised when God doesn't show up."

Nevertheless, we often say, "Tomorrow I will do this or that," or, "Next year I am going to go there on vacation," but we are not to boast about what we will do without submitting our plans to God, because none of us knows if tomorrow will even come. Notice what the apostle James writes about this:

> Now listen, you who say, "Today or tomorrow we will go to this or that city, spend a year there, carry on business and make money." Why, you do not even know what will happen tomorrow. What is your life? You are

a mist that appears for a little while and then vanishes. Instead you ought to say, "If it is the Lord's will, we will live and do this or that."

James 4:13–15

This passage makes clear that we should always care more about God's will than about what we want to do. We all make plans, but we can daily let God know that no matter what we plan, we only want to do it if it is His will.

You may remember that Proverbs 3:6 teaches us to acknowledge God in all of our ways. I don't think we need to have a long prayer session about every plan we make, but we should at least humbly say in our hearts, "Lord, I would like to do this tomorrow if You approve."

Solomon continues in Proverbs 27:2 to say: "Let someone else praise you, and not your own mouth; an outsider, and not your own lips." None of us enjoys spending time with people who constantly gloat about what they can do or have done, what they own, or who they know. Such people are often deeply insecure, and they boast in order to make themselves feel and appear to be important. We are all important to God, and we don't have to try to impress others with our achievements. Let someone else brag on you; don't do it yourself. Many people suffer from insecurity on some level, and we can help build them up by complimenting them as often as possible. Encouragement and affirmation are always appreciated.

BE HAPPY WITH YOUR LIFE

"Anger is cruel and fury overwhelming, but who can stand before jealousy?" (v. 4). We have already learned from Proverbs that envy rots the bones (Proverbs 14:30). And we know from 1 Corinthians 13:4 that love "does not envy." God wants us to rejoice when others rejoice and to mourn when they mourn (Romans 12:15). He does not want us to be jealous and envious of anyone nor, according to the tenth commandment, to covet anything other people have (Exodus 20:17). Since this instruction made the top ten, it must be very important.

I think jealousy may also be a symptom of insecurity. In my early years in ministry, I was jealous of people who had larger ministries than mine or who had opportunities that were not open to me. I learned to trust God to do what was right for me at the right time and not to compare myself to others. We should be glad for people when they are blessed, and I believe that when we are, it opens the door for God to do special things for us also.

When we are happy with the life God has given us, it honors Him. Let me urge you to beware of always wanting something that someone else has. We can want things and pray for our lives to improve if needed, but we should never be jealous of anything other people have—whether it's a job, a possession, an opportunity, a relationship, a talent, physical appearance, intellectual ability, or something else. Until we can be happy for others when they are blessed, we will not get the things we want.

Don't fall into the trap of thinking, *I wish I looked like her*, or *I wish I had a house as big as theirs*, or *I wish I had as much money as they do*. This kind of wishing does no good at all. It only serves to keep us unhappy and ungrateful for what God is doing in our lives. Wanting what someone else has can even cause us to begin to dislike and resent the person who has it. Jealousy is a waste of energy, because it never aids in helping us get what we want; it only hinders us. Learn to be content in all things and trust God to give you what is right for you at the right time.

> *Are you enjoying where you are on the way to where you are going?*

WARNING SIGNS

"The prudent see danger and take refuge, but the simple keep going and pay the penalty" (v. 12). I mentioned earlier that we often ignore warning signs that God gives us to keep us out of trouble. If the house next door to you was on fire and the blaze was getting dangerously close to your home, I'm sure you would get out of your house. However, if your back has been hurting for a year, you might be inclined to put up with the pain without ever going to the doctor to see what is wrong. The pain might be a warning sign that something more serious could develop if you don't have it checked.

About twenty-five years ago I had back pain consistently

for a long, long time. I was praying and asking God to heal me, but I refused to go to the doctor. I didn't want to take time for the appointment. I said I was trusting God to heal me, but I think I was really just being unwise. I was foolish to put off seeing the doctor for so long. The pain was warning me that something needed attention, but I ignored it. Eventually, one morning I got out of bed and couldn't walk without assistance, which forced me to get help. Because I let the situation go on too long, getting better required many chiropractic adjustments and much therapy. You may have done something like this in the past, or perhaps you are doing it now. If so, I advise you to use wisdom and take care of the situation.

Not only does God warn us, but we also receive warnings from the people around us, and we can easily miss them. If your children or spouse should say, "I feel like I never see you," or "I feel like we never talk anymore," that is a warning that they are unhappy. A wise person will correct a problem while it is still small instead of waiting until it becomes so big that it may not be able to be fixed.

God gives us discernment, which means that we should not be caught unaware of problems coming our way. We may not see every problem ahead of time, but we will see many of them if we are prudent.

Watch for the warning signs that God gives you, and be prudent so you can avoid harm, danger, or long-term negative effects.

SPEND TIME WITH PEOPLE
WHO MAKE YOU BETTER

"As iron sharpens iron, so one person sharpens another" (v. 17). This scripture could easily be passed over without our giving it much thought, but it is a wonderful scripture when we understand what it means.

Some people with whom we spend our time challenge us to be better simply by their presence and example. Others drag us down through their ways and words. The time you spend with people is precious, and I urge you not to waste time on vain and useless pursuits.

> When you think about the people you spend most of your time with, other than family, do you believe you are making the best choices you can make?

If you need to improve in an area of your life, I recommend finding people who have the character traits in which you want to grow. I enjoy spending time with people who are generous, because they inspire me to be more and more generous. I also love to spend time with people who refuse to gossip or say judgmental things about others, because that keeps me mindful of the way I use my words.

We have only a certain amount of time to invest in relationships, and we should make sure our investments are good and wise. We should put most of the time we have for relationships into the ones most important to us. Dave and I have four grown children and twelve grandchildren, and I make sure I invest time in all of those relationships, because they are very important to me.

THE JOY OF SATISFACTION

"Death and Destruction are never satisfied, and neither are human eyes" (v. 20). It seems that we are always seeing something and wishing we had it. The entire advertising industry is built on this idea and on getting us to purchase what vendors want us to buy. But we can learn to be content and thankful for what we have, while trusting God for anything else we need or desire. God invites us to ask Him for whatever we want, but we are then to wait patiently for His will to be done.

We need to beware of lusting after anything we do not have. I believe *lust* describes the feeling of wanting something so strongly that we have decided we cannot be happy without it. Lust often causes us to compromise our moral values, which is always a mistake that carries consequences we will not like. This scripture describes the source of lust:

> For everything in the world—the lust of the flesh, the lust of the eyes, and the pride of life—comes not from the Father but from the world.
>
> 1 John 2:16

Satan uses these things—the lust of the flesh, the lust of the eyes, and pride—to keep us dissatisfied, ever longing for more and more. Perhaps we should learn to look at things and enjoy them without lusting after them.

Material goods are transitory. They are here today and gone tomorrow, but God is eternal and everlasting. He has placed eternity in our hearts (Ecclesiastes 3:11), and we should long for Him, not for things. There is nothing wrong with wanting things and asking God for them, but to say we cannot be happy without them is not a godly attitude.

PROVERBS 28

Proverbs 28 begins with strong words that indicate a connection between righteousness and boldness: "The wicked flee though no one pursues, but the righteous are as bold as a lion" (v. 1). I believe that ungodly people live with underlying fear because they know deep inside that their actions are wrong. Though they may justify and make excuses for their behavior, they still know it is wrong. But righteous people do not have a guilty conscience, and this allows them to be bold and confident.

Wickedness creates many problems for the wicked, and righteousness brings many blessings to those who are righteous. God sets both before us and gives us the freedom to choose the path we will walk, but He urges us to choose life and righteousness (Deuteronomy 30:19). Having choices is fun, but the freedom to make them also carries great responsibilities.

We will have the fruit of the seeds we sow (the choices we make). We always have opportunities to make changes. If people have chosen wickedness and realize they have made the wrong choice, they can be sorry, repent for their ways, and choose to go in the right direction at any time. God's arms are always open wide to them. Those who come to Him will never be rejected.

Do what is right and enjoy a life of boldness and confidence. Do what is wrong and you will live with the hidden fear that you may be caught at any time and your ungodly ways will be revealed. If you need to make a change, don't put it off. Now is the time to begin doing what is right.

THE RESPONSIBILITY OF LEADERSHIP

Proverbs 28 includes four verses about rulers, meaning people in authority. Some people today don't think of themselves as living under a ruler, so we can also think of these verses as describing leaders. All of us can relate to having leaders.

1. "A ruler with discernment and knowledge maintains order" (v. 2).
2. "A ruler who oppresses the poor is like a driving rain that leaves no crops" (v. 3).
3. "Like a roaring lion or a charging bear is a wicked ruler over a helpless people" (v. 15).
4. "A tyrannical ruler practices extortion, but one who hates ill-gotten gain will enjoy a long reign" (v. 16).

All of these verses teach us one lesson: Leadership is not only a privilege, but it is also a responsibility. God will deal with people who hold power over others and mistreat them in any way—and they won't like it. Holding authority over people is serious business, and leaders have an obligation to represent God and treat people as He would treat them. Leaders are to be honest in all their dealings, and when they are the type of leader that God desires them to be, then those they lead will be blessed.

When I say "the type of leader that God desires them to be," I am talking about people who have the character and the heart of a godly leader, whether they are church or ministry leaders or leaders in some other sphere of society. Only people of strong character can handle responsibility wisely, especially when that responsibility affects other people's lives. Responsible leaders are people of strong, honorable character, who maintain a close personal relationship with God and walk in integrity in every area of their lives—spiritually, in marriage and family relationships, with their friends and neighbors, in their thoughts and words, in their finances, and in every other way.

Regardless of a person's area of responsibility, godly leaders also demonstrate the fruit of the Holy Spirit—"love, joy, peace, forbearance [patience], kindness, goodness, faithfulness, gentleness and self-control" (Galatians 5:22–23). They are forgiving and humble. They conduct their personal lives wisely, and they lead others according to wisdom. They do not allow their emotions to cause them to be up one moment and down the next, but they are stable and strong in the Lord.

The United States is a democracy, a country in which we get to elect our leaders. We should be well informed about the character of those we vote into office and hold them accountable to keep the promises they have made. Leaders influence other people, and we want to make sure that influence is good and beneficial.

Leadership is also an opportunity to be good to the poor and marginalized, and leaders should also care about those who are truly needy. The United States has a lot of poverty, as do other nations of the world. Proverbs urges us frequently to be good and generous to people in need, and God is watching to see how we treat them.

If you hold any kind of leadership position, realize what a privilege it is and be sure to treat everyone with fairness and integrity, regardless of their station in life. Demonstrate the qualities of a responsible leader, and maintain a strong spiritual life personally. Spend time helping others, and be assured that lifting them to a better position in life also promotes you.

HIDDEN SIN

"Whoever conceals their sins does not prosper, but the one who confesses and renounces them finds mercy" (v. 13). This reminds me of John 3:20: "Everyone who does evil hates the light." Trying to hide our sins from God is useless, because He sees and knows all. It is our secrets that make us sick. James 5:16 says we are to confess our faults to one another so that we may be healed and restored. Evil hates the light, but God is light (John 9:5), and He calls us to live in the light and be the light of the world (Matthew 5:16; 1 John 1:7). This means we cannot hide our sins and walk in God's will at the same time.

I think we experience freedom when we realize that God sees and knows all things and that nothing and no one is hidden from Him. Admitting and confessing our sins is equivalent to gathering them up and throwing them away. We give them to Jesus, and He gives us His forgiveness. What a wonderful exchange! He forgets our sins and removes them as far as the east is from the west (Psalm 103:12). If you have sin hidden in your heart, I urge you not to live one more day that way. Talk to God about it, and, if needed, speak with a trusted and spiritually mature leader or friend about it. Talking with someone else about our sins is often very helpful. As the old saying goes, "Confession is good for the soul."

> *Is there any hidden sin you need to confess to the Lord?*

Telling someone about our sin may be embarrassing, but a little embarrassment is worth the freedom we gain from no longer carrying the burden of secret sin.

THE FOLLY OF TRUSTING ONESELF

"Those who trust in themselves are fools, but those who walk in wisdom are kept safe" (v. 26). Trusting ourselves instead of trusting God is folly, because we all have weaknesses that will reveal themselves when we don't want them to. God wants us to depend on Him, not to be independent of Him.

Those who pride themselves in being able to take care

of themselves or brag about being a self-made man or a self-made woman have difficulty learning to trust God completely. Those who have been hurt and treated unjustly may also struggle in this area. As one who was abused during my childhood, I reached a point where I vowed to myself that I would never trust anyone, especially not men. My goal was to reach the point where I could take care of myself and never have to ask anyone for anything.

As a young person, whenever I asked my dad for anything, there was always a price to pay in order to get it, so I learned early in life to not need anyone. You may have encountered similar situations. However, after entering a relationship with Jesus and wanting to trust Him instead of myself, I found trust difficult simply because no one had ever taken care of me. Thankfully, He was patient with me, and He has taught me that He is the only one who is always strong and can always be trusted. We simply are not capable of running our own lives and doing a good job of it. Apart from Jesus we can do nothing (John 15:5).

For years, I experienced a great deal of frustration because my plans never seemed to work out. I did not understand this at all, because many things I tried to do were ministry-oriented and geared toward helping people. I also experienced frustration and a lack of success in trying to change myself. I heard sermons that convicted me of a need for change and tried very hard to do so, but with no success. Thankfully, I finally learned through God's Word that as long as we try to do things on our own without asking for God's help, we are destined for failure.

Now, I ask God every morning to help me in all I do that day, and I lean and rely on Him. Now, things work better. We should not make our own plans and then pray that God will make them work. Instead, we should pray for God's plan and then enjoy having Him work with us to accomplish His will.

PROVERBS 29

Most of what Solomon writes in Proverbs 29 has already been written in other parts of Proverbs, reminding us once again that repetition is important. This chapter begins with teaching about the consequences of our choices: "Whoever remains stiff-necked after many rebukes will suddenly be destroyed—without remedy" (v. 1). In this verse, Solomon warns us about the danger of being rebellious and stubborn. After having read and studied twenty-eight chapters of Proverbs while working on this book thus far, I am convinced that if people are determined to remain wicked, the only thing they can expect is destruction.

Over and over, and in many different ways, God's Word shows us that we will reap what we sow. Yet many people continue to live in opposition to His will. They do not walk in wisdom, and they have no reverential fear of God. Why they choose to live this way is a mystery to me. Who would deliberately choose a life of misery and destruction when a life of blessedness and joy is available? Apparently, those who are unwise do choose to live this way. They continue to think they can do what is wrong and somehow get good results, but that is impossible.

Throughout Proverbs 29, Solomon compares the righteous and the results of their lives with the wicked and the results of their lives. "When the righteous thrive, the people rejoice; when the wicked rule, the people groan" (v. 2). Making right choices not only affects us, it also has an impact on those around us. Similarly, making wrong choices also influences our lives and the people around us. As parents, our right choices will leave lasting effects on our children.

I understand this because my parents made evil choices, which had a very bad influence on my brother and me. When I had children, I did not want them to have the same experience. Dave and I have four children, and they have thanked us many times for making the right choices we made, because of how those choices have positively affected their lives.

> When you make choices, do you consider how they can have a positive influence on the people who are close to you?

One person can have an amazing influence over many. The Bible says that through Adam's sin many became sinners, and through Jesus' sacrifice of obedience many were made righteous (Romans 5:19). Be sure you make choices that will have a positive, godly effect on your children, other family members, friends, and associates.

Proverbs 29:6 says, "Evildoers are snared by their own sin," meaning that they are trapped by their wrong choices. Verse 6 continues: "but the righteous shout for joy and are glad." After living many years, I have concluded that the main thing most people want is simply to be happy. God's Word is clear about the behavior and choices that will produce the joy people desire.

When ungodly people sin, they may thrive for a period of time, "but the righteous will see their downfall" (v. 16). The harvest of our thoughts, words, and actions may take a while to come in, but it always comes, whether good or evil. Righteous people may have to be patient for a long time to see the rewards of following God, and those who do evil may seem to flourish for a season. But we need to remember that the reward of wickedness will surely come, as will the reward of righteousness. Remember, wise people do now what they will be happy with later—and later always comes. Keep making good choices even if it does not appear to be producing a good harvest in the moment. In due time, it will.

JUSTICE FOR THE POOR

In this chapter, as in many others, Solomon writes about the proper way to treat the poor. "The righteous care about justice for the poor, but the wicked have no such concern" (v. 7). Selfishness and wickedness always go hand in hand, so we should not be surprised when ungodly people are insensitive toward the needy. Contrast this with Proverbs 29:14, which says, "If a king judges the poor with fairness, his throne will be established forever," and you will be reminded of how important our treatment of the less fortunate is to God.

The Old Testament figure Job made sure that he cared for the poor. He "rescued the poor who cried for help, and the fatherless who had none to assist them" (Job 29:12). He made the widow's heart sing for joy (Job 29:13). Then he said, "I put on righteousness" (Job 29:14). We are made the righteousness of God through our faith in Christ (2 Corinthians 5:21), but to "put on righteousness" means to take action to do what is right.

Job continued to rehearse a long list of ways he helped those in need and concluded by saying that had he not done them, "then let my arm fall from the shoulder, let it be broken off at the joint" (Job 31:22). What a strong statement this is! He is saying that if we don't use our arms to help others, we have no need for them. They are useless and should be broken off of our bodies. I think we can safely say that God is serious about His instructions concerning how we should treat the poor.

Paul's life offers another good example of treating the poor well. After his conversion to Christ, he ministered either alone or with Barnabas for many years before meeting with the apostles in Jerusalem. He had visited Peter once, but that was all. After he met with the apostles to see if they approved of what he was preaching, they told him they approved of everything. Their only comment was to remind him not to forget the poor (Galatians 2:10). Paul, of course, was helping the poor and was glad to continue doing so. I have always thought it interesting that of everything the apostles could have said to Paul, they chose to remind him to help the poor. I think this shows how important it is for us to notice those in need and treat them with compassion.

DON'T BE AFRAID OF WHAT OTHER
PEOPLE WILL THINK

The phrase *the fear of man* has been used in Christianity for years to describe the unhealthy fear of what other people may think of us, say about us, or do to us. It is not related to a fear of men in general, but perhaps to the fear of their rejection, criticism, or judgment. The Bible does use the term *fear of man*, and I have used it frequently in my teaching, so it is important for us to know what it means and doesn't mean. When we fear other people, we give them a measure of control over us, and that is not how God wants us to live. He wants us to allow the Holy Spirit—not the fear of what someone else may think or how other people will respond—to lead and guide us and to direct our decisions.

Proverbs 29:25 says, "Fear of man will prove to be a snare, but whoever trusts in the Lord is kept safe." We must choose between being people-pleasers and being God-pleasers—we cannot be both. The fear of man leads many people astray and away from the will of God. Being intimidated or afraid of other people's rejection or of what they think of us is something that we should steadfastly resist. Paul writes that he would not have become an apostle of Jesus Christ if he had tried to be popular with people (Galatians 1:10). We can learn from this comment that in order to serve God and live in the center of His will, people will often be displeased with us.

People want us to do what they want and what gives them

pleasure, but God calls us to follow Him, no matter what it costs us. Jesus wasn't popular with many people around Him, but He didn't allow their opinions to control His choices. When God called me into ministry, many of my friends and family members rejected me because they thought what I was doing was wrong. They didn't think I was qualified to teach God's Word, nor was it popular at that time for a woman to be in ministry. Those people were right about my qualifications. Educationally speaking, I was not qualified, but God's anointing is what qualifies us, not a person's stamp of approval. As of the writing of this book, I have been in ministry almost forty-five years, and God has blessed our ministry to be able to help many people. I cannot imagine how miserable my life would have been had I chosen to please people instead of pleasing God.

> *Do you often make decisions based on what other people think or say you should do?*

I urge you to always follow God even if He leads you into something that people disapprove of or do not understand. I think that the devil uses the fear of rejection to keep us out of God's will. However, if we disobey God in order to please people, those very people will end up rejecting us for something anyway, and we will have missed our opportunity with God. Remember, Proverbs 29:25 teaches us that the fear of man is a trap, but if we trust in God, we will be kept safe.

PROVERBS 30

Proverbs 30 is not a collection of Solomon's sayings, and we can easily see that someone other than Solomon wrote it by simply looking at the change in the style of writing. This chapter comes from the wisdom of a man named Agur, the son of Jakeh. Little is known about him, but we can tell from Proverbs 30 that he was a wise and observant person.

In the first six verses of Proverbs 30, Agur speaks of his weakness as a man, especially in comparison to God's greatness. Agur is still learning from the God who knows everything and whose Word is flawless (v. 5). This is a wonderful example for us to follow. No matter how much we learn, God can always teach us more.

"TWO THINGS I ASK OF YOU, LORD"

Agur makes two requests of the Lord and does not want God to refuse them before he dies (v. 7). In verse 8, he asks the Lord to keep falsehood and lies far from him. I have often said that we should pray daily not to be deceived. Apparently this was important to Agur, because it was one of his two requests of the Lord. Falsehood, lies, deception, and dishonesty cause all kinds of trouble and lead people into bondage. Only the truth makes us free (John 8:32).

Agur also asks God to give him neither poverty nor riches, but only his daily bread. He knew that if God gave him more than his daily allotment, he might have too much and disown the Lord or become poor and steal and dishonor the name of God. I am especially impressed by this request to have neither riches nor poverty. Many people do ask for riches, but they would not always be good for them. I have prayed that God would only give me what I can handle and still keep Him first in my life. This, in essence, is Agur's request. His prayers were wise, and ours should be also.

"THREE THINGS THAT ARE NEVER SATISFIED"

Agur begins this section including Proverbs 30:15–16 by saying, "There are three things that are never satisfied, four that never say, 'Enough!'" (v. 15). The grave is never satisfied because it always claims another victim. The barren womb is never satisfied because it was created to bear children. Land is never satisfied because it dries out and becomes thirsty for more water. No matter how much water the land gets, it will always need more. And fire never says, "Enough!" because it consumes anything and everything it touches. It will keep burning unless it is put out.

These sayings are interesting to say the least, and they

deserve some thought on our part. These are earthly things that can never be satisfied. But in Christ, we can be satisfied completely. Contentment and satisfaction are wonderful, while constantly wanting something else no matter how much we have only makes us miserable. Perhaps Agur wants us to think about the misery of never being satisfied compared to the joy of satisfaction.

One of the best-known passages in the Bible regarding contentment is in Philippians 4:11–12. Paul writes: "*I have learned to be content whatever the circumstances. I know what it is to be in need, and I know what it is to have plenty. I have learned the secret of being content in any and every situation, whether well fed or hungry, whether living in plenty or in want*" (emphasis mine). Paul wrote these words about contentment while in prison. We can be sure that his circumstances there

> *Have you found contentment in Christ?*

were extremely difficult. But he chose to be content, and he found his contentment in his relationship with Jesus Christ. You and I have that same opportunity. As believers in Christ, no matter what our circumstances, we can also choose to be content in Him.

THREE THINGS THAT ARE AMAZING

Agur writes of "three things that are too amazing for me, four that I do not understand" (v. 18). He lists them in verse 19.

"The way of an eagle in the sky" is truly amazing. How do these magnificent birds glide through the sky and stay in the air with nothing holding them up? They do it by God's power, and their flight is truly amazing and beautiful. We would be increasingly astounded by all that God can do if we took more time to study the aspects of His creation that we cannot understand with the natural mind.

The second thing Agur mentions is "the way of a snake on a rock." Like many people, I don't like snakes. But if I think about the way they glide across rocks and fields and yet have no legs, I am amazed. How do they do it? The way they are able to move can only be credited to God's design.

"The way of a ship on the high seas" is also too amazing to understand. How can something so huge and heavy not sink in the water? How can it remain upright against terrible storms with high winds and waves? Truly, the creative genius that God has given to people to enable them to create such remarkable things is awesome.

The fourth thing that Agur mentions in verse 19 is "the way of a man with a young woman." He is speaking of the two making love. In our society sex has in many respects been portrayed in ways that would not be considered beautiful, but in its pure form it is truly amazing. It is so amazing and beautiful that it is no wonder the devil has attempted to ruin its beauty by causing people to use it for abusive purposes.

"UNDER THREE THINGS
THE EARTH TREMBLES"

Agur observes, "Under three things the earth trembles, under four it cannot bear up" (v. 21). I think his meaning here is that these things will always cause trouble on earth, and those who dwell on earth will have to deal with them. No matter how hard anyone tries to make these things work well, they will never produce anything positive.

The first thing Agur mentions is "a servant who becomes king" (v. 22). He will never have the wisdom to rule. If a servant were to be elevated to the position of king, he would be in a position beyond his gifting and ability. He would make bad decisions and cause trouble for as long as he tried to rule.

We should not try to do things that are beyond our ability to do well. People who do this are very unhappy. They are frustrated and live with a great deal of stress. Most of us have tried this in certain ways. We have compared ourselves with other people and wanted to do what they do, or have the position they have, only to find that what may be easy for someone else can be nearly impossible for us.

Stay within your God-given abilities and you will be successful and at ease. Let me balance this by saying that it is not wrong to try new things. In fact, I encourage you to be adventurous, because it is one way to find out what your abilities are. When you identify your strengths, work to develop them.

Agur states that the earth also trembles under "a godless fool who gets plenty to eat" (v. 22). When people are
physically or spiritually hungry they become willing to do
just about anything to satisfy their hunger. If a fool, however,
gets plenty to satisfy him, he will never seek for more. If we
need to change in some way in order to be more like Jesus,
we won't seek that change unless we feel dissatisfied with
what we are. I have learned that if I start feeling dissatisfied
for no apparent reason, God is probably trying to deal with
me about something, and I just need to spend time with Him
and find out what it is.

Next is "a contemptible woman who gets married" (v. 23).
A woman who is contemptible, meaning hateful or deserving
of contempt, had her own problems when she was single,
but now that she is married, she causes trouble for her family
also. The agony one person can cause if they are wicked and
foolish is staggering. My father was that way, and the number
of people he made miserable is too many to count.

The last thing that Agur mentions in this section is "a servant who displaces her mistress" (v. 23). In order for a servant
to do so, she has to be devious, deceptive, and conniving.
She probably pretends to love her mistress, but all the while
she is scheming behind her back to displace her and take her
position.

A woman who once worked with me wanted my position
as teacher of the ladies' meeting at our church. She caused a
great deal of trouble through spreading rumors and making
sly remarks that caused people to be suspicious of me.

If you live wisely, you will never try to promote yourself,

especially if it means displacing someone else in order to do it. True promotion comes from the Lord, and if it is God's will for you to have a position, He will give it to you at the right time.

FOUR THINGS ARE SMALL, BUT EXTREMELY WISE

In Proverbs 30:24–28, Agur names four things that are small, yet wise: ants, hyraxes, locusts, and lizards.

Ants are tiny creatures that have "little strength, yet they store up their food in the summer" (v. 25). Proverbs 6:7–8 says that they work hard without an overseer to gather their food at harvest time (when it is accessible), so they don't go hungry when food is not available.

Hyraxes, mentioned in Proverbs 30:26, are small animals found in Africa and the Middle East. These furry, four-legged mammals are also called rock badgers. Agur tells us that although they are small and have little power, they are wise enough to know how to survive by making their homes in the crags of rocks.

"Locusts have no king, yet they advance together in ranks" (v. 27). It is amazing that they work together so they can move forward without having anyone to rule over them.

"A lizard can be caught with the hand, yet it is found in kings' palaces" (v. 28). How many people would love to be found in the king's palace but have not been invited? Yet the tiny lizard can get in anytime it wants to gain access.

Truly God has made marvelous things that we cannot understand with our natural minds, and we should take time to notice them, ponder them, and let them amaze us.

THREE THINGS THAT ARE STATELY

To be stately (v. 29) means to have a dignified manner or to be majestic in appearance or manner. Agur says, "There are three things that are stately in their stride, four that move with stately bearing." They are "a lion, mighty among beasts, who retreats before nothing; a strutting rooster, a he-goat, and a king secure against revolt" (vv. 30–31).

The lion has been called the king of beasts and has long symbolized royalty and courage. The boldness of the lion enables this creature to retreat "before nothing." Every other animal backs down when facing a lion.

When I read about the rooster, I remember that my grandfather had a rooster that strutted about as though he were king of the barnyard. Roosters are often mean. One day the rooster attacked me, and that night, we ate him for dinner.

A he-goat is said to have a stately walk but is also very aggressive. These male goats want something but behave in a manner that often prevents them from having it. Unwise people are the same way. They go about trying to get what they want in a way that will actually prevent them from obtaining their desired results.

And last, a king is stately by nature, and one who has worked to make sure his kingdom is secure against revolt

is wise indeed. It is always good to do preventative mainte-
nance rather than waiting until a disaster is upon us to take
any action. The wise king thinks ahead and gets prepared just
in case a revolt arises.

Using people, animals, and situations in the natural
world, Agur teaches us lessons of wisdom. His style is different than Solomon's, but it is effective. Everything he presents
causes us to consider truths we might not otherwise ponder
and to learn helpful, practical lessons from his insights.

PROVERBS 31

Proverbs 31, like Proverbs 30, is not a chapter that Solomon wrote. It contains the sayings of King Lemuel. Lemuel is not mentioned among the kings of Israel or Judah, so we know little about him. We do know, however, that he learned the wisdom he shares in this chapter from his mother and desired to pass it on to others.

Proverbs 31:1–9 includes various teachings on several subjects. In verse 3, King Lemuel's mother instructs him not to spend his strength on women or his "vigor on those who ruin kings." In other words, she teaches him to use wisdom concerning the way he exerts his energy and to be careful about those with whom he spends his time and develops relationships. This is good advice for all of us.

> Do you use wisdom in relationships?

Verses 4–7 focus on habits involving alcohol. King Lemuel's mother says that kings should not drink wine or crave beer, "lest they drink and forget what has been decreed, and deprive all the oppressed of their rights" (v. 5). According to her, beer is "for those who are perishing" and "wine for those who are in anguish!" (v. 6). And verse 7 states that those people drink in order to forget their problems and their misery. I have addressed the subject of alcohol previously in this book and encouraged everyone to seek the Lord personally regarding its use. I will say here, though, that unless people are able to put limits on themselves, they should not drink alcohol. Those who do consume it should do so only in moderation.

Verses 8–9 encourage us to "speak up for those who cannot speak for themselves," and urge us to "defend the rights of the poor and needy." We are not only to help the poor personally but also to work to bring justice to them so they will not be needy for the rest of their lives. Proverbs frequently mentions the importance of helping the poor, and I think it is fitting that this important topic comes up again in the last chapter of the book, this time from someone other than Solomon.

THE WIFE OF NOBLE CHARACTER

The Proverbs 31 woman is quite a role model for godly women. She is called "a wife of noble character" in the NIV (v. 10). Other translations refer to her as "a virtuous wife" (NKJV), "a capable, intelligent, and virtuous woman" (AMPC), and "an excellent wife" (ESV). However, with all these accolades, I think she has also caused many women to feel they are missing the mark as wives. This woman seems to be absolutely perfect, but perhaps she is the ideal rather than someone who actually existed. King Lemuel's mother may have been presenting her desire for what his wife should be like, but one thing is certain: The woman described in Proverbs 31 is amazing, and she is an excellent example.

Such a high-quality woman as the one described in Proverbs 31 is hard to find and far more valuable than rubies, which are well known as precious jewels (v. 10). "Her husband has full confidence in her and lacks nothing of value. She brings him good, not harm, all the days of her life" (vv. 11–12).

This ideal woman is a hard worker, and she provides a variety of good foods for her family to enjoy (v. 14). She gets up early, even before daylight, and prepares "food for her family and portions for her female servants" (v. 15). The Amplified Bible, Classic Edition indicates in this verse that she gets up early to gain spiritual strength as well as to make provisions for the day. I believe a good wife must spend time with God before she begins the rest of her day if she expects it to go well.

She is also skilled in business matters (vv. 16–18). She thinks about the investments she is considering making before she takes action on them and reviews her current responsibilities before taking on more.

She also stays up late at night and makes clothing for her family (vv. 13, 18–19). I tried once to make my family some clothes, and I can promise you, they were not wearable when I finished. I am very thankful that we now have many shopping sites from which to choose clothing for our families.

Remember, the Proverbs 31 woman is an ideal. All of us probably will not be able to do everything she does or have all the gifts she has. I don't sew, and if you can't sew either, that is okay.

The Proverbs 31 woman is generous to the poor and needy (v. 20). During bad weather, her family has no need to fear because she prepares for it ahead of time and makes sure they have what they need to protect them (v. 21). She makes covers for her bed and is personally clothed in fine linen and purple (v. 22). In Bible times, the color purple was associated with royalty.

Her husband is respected because of his fine wife (v. 23). She makes linen garments and sells them, so she not only works hard at home but is also involved in earning income for the family (v. 24). She is a woman of "strength and dignity," and she is so secure that she can laugh at any trouble that may be looming in the days ahead (v. 25).

This woman "speaks with wisdom, and faithful instruction is on her tongue" (v. 26). I especially like the Amplified Bible, Classic Edition's rendering of this verse, because it says that "the law of kindness" is on her tongue. Whenever we have a chance to speak or show kindness to others, we should do so. Kindness is a fruit of the Holy Spirit (Galatians 5:22).

The Proverbs 31 woman is not idle (v. 27). Other words for *idle* include *unproductive* and *useless*. A woman who is not idle is diligent and industrious. She is not lazy; she does things that are useful. The children of a noble wife "arise and call her blessed" (v. 28). Her husband "praises her" and says to her, "Many women do noble things, but you surpass them all" (vv. 28–29). It is good for husbands to remember to praise, compliment, and appreciate their wives. This will keep them encouraged. However, if any woman has a husband who is not very encouraging, she still has a responsibility to behave in a godly manner, while praying for her husband to show more appreciation for her.

"Charm is deceptive, and beauty is fleeting," but a woman such as the one described in Proverbs 31 "is to be praised" (v. 30). She has more than outward beauty; she is beautiful in her inner being also. She should be honored for all that she has done, and her works will "bring her praise" (v. 31).

This noble wife is admirable and presents a good example for us to follow. Godly women would be wise to receive her description as a guideline for their lives. However, not everyone has the same abilities, and some women may have to find a pathway that is bit different from the one our Proverbs 31 woman took. For example, she provided a variety of good foods for her family. I provide for my family also, but I buy most of it at a restaurant and take it home rather than cooking it myself. I also know several women who are simply not good cooks, so their husbands prepare the meals. You can be a good wife without doing everything the way most people do it, so don't feel belittled if you are not exactly like the woman that Proverbs 31 describes.

CONCLUSION

This concludes the teaching from the Book of Proverbs. It is so filled with wisdom that to mention each point would require an exhaustive book that most people would not read. As I mentioned in the introduction, I have taken what I felt led of the Holy Spirit to highlight and I encourage you to study this book along with the writings of Proverbs for yourself. I am sure you will find topics and insights that are important to you that I did not specifically address.

I'm also sure that as you pray for wisdom, the Holy Spirit will lead you to certain verses and principles in Proverbs that apply to the specific situations in your life. Proverbs contains thirty-one chapters, and some people read one chapter of Proverbs for every day of a thirty-one day month (two on the last day of a thirty-day month). While this approach is effective for some people and you may want to do it, I would also encourage you to ask God to lead you each day to any wisdom He wants to reveal to you from this book. Its wisdom will guide you faithfully over the course of your lifetime.

This book is intentionally titled *In Search of Wisdom*. The search is necessary and important. Though I have mentioned this previously, I want to emphasize here that wisdom is a treasure, and only those who seek it find it.

I hope you have gleaned much practical wisdom for the many areas of life that Proverbs covers, especially its seven foundational principles: wisdom, understanding, prudence, knowledge, discretion, discernment, and the fear of the Lord. I pray you have been helped and encouraged by this book and that you will read it often to stay refreshed in all the principles that it teaches.

Do you have a real relationship with Jesus?

God loves you! He created you to be a special, unique, one-of-a-kind individual, and He has a specific purpose and plan for your life. And through a personal relationship with your Creator—God—you can discover a way of life that will truly satisfy your soul.

No matter who you are, what you've done, or where you are in your life right now, God's love and grace are greater than your sin— your mistakes. Jesus willingly gave His life so you can receive forgiveness from God and have new life in Him. He's just waiting for you to invite Him to be your Savior and Lord.

If you are ready to commit your life to Jesus and follow Him, all you have to do is ask Him to forgive your sins and give you a fresh start in the life you are meant to live. Begin by praying this prayer . . .

*Lord Jesus, thank You for giving Your life
for me and forgiving me of my sins so I can have
a personal relationship with You. I am sincerely
sorry for the mistakes I've made, and I know
I need You to help me live right.*

*Your Word says in Romans 10:9, "If you declare
with your mouth, 'Jesus is Lord,' and believe in
your heart that God raised him from the dead,
you will be saved" (NIV). I believe You are the Son
of God and confess You as my Savior and Lord.
Take me just as I am, and work in my heart,
making me the person You want me to be.
I want to live for You, Jesus, and I am so grateful
that You are giving me a fresh start in my
new life with You today.*

I love You, Jesus!

It's so amazing to know that God loves us so much! He wants to have a deep, intimate relationship with us that grows every day as we spend time with Him in prayer and Bible study. And we want to encourage you in your new life in Christ.

Please visit joycemeyer.org/salvation to request Joyce's book *A New Way of Living*, which is our gift to you. We also have other free resources online to help you make progress in pursuing everything God has for you.

Congratulations on your fresh start in your life in Christ! We hope to hear from you soon.

ABOUT THE AUTHOR

JOYCE MEYER is one of the world's leading practical Bible teachers. A *New York Times* bestselling author, Joyce's books have helped millions of people find hope and restoration through Jesus Christ. Joyce's programs, *Enjoying Everyday Life* and *Everyday Answers with Joyce Meyer*, air around the world on television, radio, and the Internet. Through Joyce Meyer Ministries, Joyce teaches internationally on a number of topics with a particular focus on how the Word of God applies to our everyday lives. Her candid communication style allows her to share openly and practically about her experiences so others can apply what she has learned to their lives.

Joyce has authored more than one hundred books, which have been translated into more than one hundred languages, and over 65 million of her books have been distributed worldwide. Bestsellers include *Power Thoughts*; *The Confident Woman*; *Look Great, Feel Great*; *Starting Your Day Right*; *Ending Your Day Right*; *Approval Addiction*; *How to Hear from God*; *Beauty for Ashes*; and *Battlefield of the Mind*.

Joyce's passion to help hurting people is foundational to the vision of Hand of Hope, the missions arm of Joyce Meyer Ministries. Hand of Hope provides worldwide humanitarian outreaches such as feeding programs, medical care, orphanages, disaster response, human trafficking intervention and rehabilitation, and much more—always sharing the love and gospel of Christ.

JOYCE MEYER MINISTRIES

U.S. & FOREIGN OFFICE ADDRESSES

Joyce Meyer Ministries
P.O. Box 655
Fenton, MO 63026
USA
(636) 349-0303

**Joyce Meyer Ministries—
Canada**
P.O. Box 7700
Vancouver, BC V6B 4E2
Canada
(800) 868-1002

**Joyce Meyer Ministries—
Australia**
Locked Bag 77
Mansfield Delivery Centre
Queensland 4122
Australia
(07) 3349 1200

**Joyce Meyer Ministries—
England**
P.O. Box 1549
Windsor SL4 1GT
United Kingdom
01753 831102

**Joyce Meyer Ministries—
South Africa**
P.O. Box 5
Cape Town 8000
South Africa
(27) 21-701-1056

**Joyce Meyer Ministries—
Francophonie**
29 avenue Maurice Chevalier
77330 Ozoir la Ferriere
France

**Joyce Meyer Ministries—
Germany**
Postfach 761001
22060 Hamburg
Germany
+49 (0)40 / 88 88 4 11 11

**Joyce Meyer Ministries—
Netherlands**
Lorenzlaan 14
7002 HB Doetinchem
+31 657 555 9789

**Joyce Meyer Ministries—
Russia**
P.O. Box 789
Moscow 101000
Russia
+7 (495) 727-14-68

OTHER BOOKS BY JOYCE MEYER

Power Thoughts
Power Thoughts Devotional
Quiet Times with God Devotional
Reduce Me to Love
The Secret Power of Speaking
God's Word
The Secrets of Spiritual Power
The Secret to True Happiness
Seven Things That Steal Your Joy
Start Your New Life Today
Starting Your Day Right
Straight Talk
Teenagers Are People Too!
Trusting God Day by Day
The Word, the Name, the Blood
Woman to Woman
You Can Begin Again
Your Battles Belong to the Lord*

JOYCE MEYER SPANISH TITLES

Belleza en Lugar de Cenizas
(Beauty for Ashes)
Buena Salud, Buena Vida
(Good Health, Good Life)
Cambia Tus Palabras, Cambia Tu Vida
(Change Your Words, Change Your Life)
El Campo de Batalla de la Mente
(Battlefield of the Mind)
Como Formar Buenos Habitos y Romper
Malos Habitos (Making Good Habits,
Breaking Bad Habits)
La Conexión de la Mente
(The Mind Connection)
Dios No Está Enojado Contigo
(God Is Not Mad at You)

La Dosis de Aprobación
(The Approval Fix)
Efesios: Comentario Biblico (Ephesians:
Biblical Commentary)
Empezando Tu Día Bien
(Starting Your Day Right)
Hágalo con Miedo (Do It Afraid)
Hazte un Favor a Ti Mismo…Perdona
(Do Yourself a Favor…Forgive)
Madre Segura de Sí Misma
(The Confident Mom)
Momentos de Quietud con Dios (Quiet
Times with God Devotional)
Pensamientos de Poder
(Power Thoughts)
Sanidad para el Alma de una Mujer
(Healing the Soul of a Woman)
Santiago: Comentario Bíblico (James:
Biblical Commentary)
Sobrecarga (Overload)*
Sus Batallas Son del Señor (Your Battles
Belong to the Lord)
Termina Bien Tu Día
(Ending Your Day Right)
Usted Puede Comenzar de Nuevo
(You Can Begin Again)
Viva Valientemente
(Living Courageously)

BOOKS BY DAVE MEYER

Life Lines

* Study Guide available for this title